JOSEPH MATTERA

KINGDOM

AWAKENING

BOOKS BY JOSEPH MATTERA

Kingdom Revolution

AVAILABLE FROM DESTINY IMAGE PUBLISHERS

JOSEPH MATTERA

KINGDOM
AWAKENING

a BLUEPRINT *for* PERSONAL
and CULTURAL TRANSFORMATION

DESTINY IMAGE® PUBLISHERS, INC.
P.O. Box 310, Shippensburg, PA 17257-0310
"Speaking to the Purposes of God for This Generation and for the Generations to Come."

This book and all other Destiny Image, Revival Press, MercyPlace, Fresh Bread, Destiny Image Fiction, and Treasure House books are available at Christian bookstores and distributors worldwide.

For a U.S. bookstore nearest you, call 1-800-722-6774.
For more information on foreign distributors, call 717-532-3040.
Reach us on the Internet: www.destinyimage.com.

Trade Paper ISBN 13: 978-0-7684-3264-0
Hardcover ISBN 978-0-7684-3479-8
Large Print ISBN 978-0-7684-3480-4
Ebook ISBN 978-0-7684-9101-2

For Worldwide Distribution, Printed in the U.S.A.
1 2 3 4 5 6 7 8 9 10 11 / 13 12 11 10

ENDORSEMENTS

The hour is late, and the situation is urgent. Among the voices wrestling the bear of societal transformation down to the ground, Joseph Mattera stands out. He is among the most substantial thinkers and communicators of this subject in the nation, if not the world. His commitment to putting ideas to the test in the real-life laboratory of New York marks him as a writer to take seriously. This book is a *must read!*

Lance Wallnau
President, Lance Learning Group
www.lancelearning.com

Talk is cheap. Many talk. But action—especially when Holy Spirit infused—means something! Action counts! Joseph Mattera—as both a leading pastor and as a bishop in the true biblical meaning of the word—not only "talks the talk," but "walks the walk." His impact in New York City and beyond is significant as he courageously and tirelessly brings the body of Christ together, instructing and modeling on how to become truly Salt and Light to his great city. The strategies found in this book come from a seasoned and successful practitioner. They will impact you—in your city. Read this!

Dr. James L. Garlow
Senior Pastor, Skyline Wesleyan Church
San Diego, California

Kingdom Awakening by Dr. Joseph Mattera is truly a revolutionary call to church leaders. Most books on the Kingdom of God, the seven mountains, and dominion are written by a teacher-theorist. Not this book! It is written by a field general who lives on the battlefield of New York City. Dr. Mattera writes as a pragmatist who is partnering with leaders from the church, political, and economic sections for the Kingdom Revolution. This book is a revelational and informational journey we all must embark upon for the cause of the King and His Kingdom. Everyone needs to read this so they too can lead His Revolution!

Dr. John P. Kelly
CEO, International Christian Wealth Builders Foundation
CEO, Leadership Education for Advancement
and Development

Finally, a book that combines passion with perspective and renewing the mind with refreshing our communities and culture. This is that rare read that case studies how the Kingdom of God works in the raw setting of New York City. Written by renowned thinker, theologian, activist, and revolutionary Joseph Mattera, it resonates with anyone who is done with groupthink and sound-byte opinions. I am so much more hopeful for our churches and cities because of this compelling read.

Dr. Joseph Umidi
Professor, Regent University

Dr. Joseph Mattera captures the call to the Church in *Kingdom Awakening*. The Church was never instructed to wait for the world to come to them. Jesus said to go, baptize, and make disciples. The transformation of our communities or counties and ultimately our country will occur when we take the torch of truth and light the way to serve those around us in the name of our Savior and Lord Jesus Christ.

Tony Perkins
President, The Family Research Council

After a century of a bifurcated Gospel, God is awakening His Church to reconnect His Gospel for both eternal life and effective living. Joe Mattera started his ministry to be in the middle of this movement of God in the middle of New York City, one of the most visible and challenged cities in the world. *Kingdom Awakening* tells this story through Joe Mattera's authentic, real-life work in networking leaders in New York's political, economic and spiritual sectors. Real transformation happened. Real lives were changed. A local church was the real source of it all. *Kingdom Awakening* tells this story with principles that apply to all of us.

Books are often either theoretical or pragmatic. *Kingdom Awakening* uniquely connects theology with practical application, with the authentic story of how one church did it well in New York City.

Brad Smith, President
Bakke Graduate University
800-935-4723
www.bgu.edu

CONTENTS

FOREWORD

Joseph Mattera, in his first book, *Kingdom Revolution*, did us all an enormous favor in moving the Kingdom of God from doctrine to doing, from the conceptual to the practical. In doing so, he is providing in New York City a model as to how the Kingdom of God may be applied for all the world to see.

No area of study is entirely valid until it is demonstrated. We don't "get it" until we become part and parcel of its dynamics. Since the Kingdom of God embraces the entire scope of redemption and thus the total work of the Church, it must be vividly and vitally demonstrated.

Now, in his second book, *Kingdom Awakening*, the concepts of the Kingdom are strengthened and the book moves on toward more transcendent involvement in the whole of community relationships and dynamics. All proper teaching and doctrine will powerfully touch the entirety of God's work, from personal relationships to all the corporate structures in society. Over the years, improvements will come, and fresh ideas will affect refinement. Mattera shows that the ideas outlined in this book will work because they have worked and are working right now in New York City.

Mattera walks us with him step by careful step through the initiatives that won trust between spiritual leaders in his area, outlining the development of methods for implementation while declaring core values that must penetrate all involved. Seeing a movement or a plan in progress is fun, but seeing the Kingdom breaking through in personal and corporate life is more than fun—it is exciting and consuming!

This grace-soaked work will revolutionize how we view the Church, how we *do* Church, and how we relate as spiritual leaders in our surroundings. Thank you, Joseph, for being a pacesetter and a planner as well as a guide for us. The book fills a vital niche in a wide-open area, and it answers the question about what it will look like when the Kingdom comes in our town.

We need a revolution, but not just any revolution will do. We have at least a dozen knee-jerk reactions to the many inexcusable flaws and indefensible shortcomings of what we presently call "church," and the fallout from most of them is horrific. Thousands are leaving the church because of feelings they cannot describe, looking for something they cannot define, with dreams and desires they cannot articulate. Many are bored, bothered, disgusted, distressed, and dry. *This revolution-awakening must be love-driven and power-demonstrated.* Our voices, for the most part, will prove quiet and confident, our walk deliberate, sheathed in humility and cautiously directional with periodic punctuations of face-to-the-floor desperation. Nothing short of this will prove able to deliver us from the maelstrom in which we find ourselves.

This volume, *Kingdom Awakening*, should be read by every person who believes that most modern expressions of the Church must be revised. It is not only an excellent read but could also well be the equivalent of the "shot heard round the world." It calls us to be Kingdomized on our knees, causing us to rise and stand with the humble prayer given us from above, *"Our Father in Heaven, Your name be hallowed, Your Kingdom come, Your will be done on earth as it is in Heaven."* According to the structure of that sentence, *"Your Kingdom come, Your will be done,"* and all other verbs contained in the prayer, we can expect what we pray for to begin immediately from the very piece of real estate on which we stand, kneel, or lay prostrate. We will delightfully move from touching our knees to the ground in passionate intercession, to standing to our feet in intense conviction, to walking out the plans of Heaven on earth in calm, determined confidence.

Joseph, no one who reads this book should ever glibly pray that prayer again without thanking God and you for this well-done masterpiece that shows us what the Kingdom might look like as it comes to the Big Apple and to our hamlet, village, town, or metropolis! It's going to happen, that's for sure! This may prove to be a simple "how-to" manual for all of us as we address ourselves to the ultimate revolution.

Jack Taylor
Dimensions Ministries
Melbourne, Florida

INTRODUCTION

BEYOND REVOLUTION
TO AWAKENING

Prior to the 1776 American Revolution, the 13 original colonies experienced the "First Great Awakening," led by the preaching of George Whitfield, John Wesley, Jonathan Edwards, and other Evangelical preachers from 1739 to 1744. Whitfield's extensive traveling throughout this burgeoning new nation was especially effective in uniting the colonies under God, which paved the way for their stand against the tyranny of King George of England. Consequently, this Christ-centered awakening led to the colonies approving the Declaration of Independence in which they officially cut their ties to the king so they could have religious, economic, and political freedom. The influence of these Evangelical preachers and numerous other colonial pastors led many to call George Whitfield "the father of the American Revolution" and the British to call this uprising, "The Parson's (clergy) Rebellion." Thus, even in American history, we see that awakening precedes revolution.

In this sequel to my first book, *Kingdom Revolution,* I deal with the Kingdom Awakening that precedes the revolution and comes when believers join hands, birthing Spirit-inspired, synergistic strategies sufficient to transform their communities. What we are speaking about is a revolution of love prompted by a Holy Spirit awakening to serve. The starting point for the Kingdom Awakening is the cultural commission in Genesis 1:28-29 in which God commissions His people to steward the earth. We must take note here that Genesis 1:29 implies that we are not to have dominion over people but over the created order. The New Testament counterpart to this passage is John 13:1-15 where Jesus demonstrated that the way to lead and have influence with people is to serve them.

It concerns me when I hear Christians talk about "taking their cities." We are not called to "take" or "buy" our cities but to "reach" our cities by serving in every realm of society with a spirit of excellence. In a post-Christian, postmodern, humanistic society, our model for cultural transformation must be the prophet Daniel, who gained prominence and became the second-in-command under the king of Babylon by serving his city with excellence and wisdom. Even though he was trained in all the wisdom, literature, and magic arts of Babylon, we have no record of him denouncing the king or the pagan culture he lived in; he simply immersed himself in his city and waited on God to give him a divine opportunity to minister. His platform to minister was not his gift of interpreting dreams or prophecy but his internal integrity, fidelity to God, and love for fellow humans. He remained faithful to God by doing his job better than anybody else until God set him up with a divine opportunity to minister to the king during his personal crisis. (See Daniel 2-4.)

Unfortunately, many leaders use Elijah rebuking King Ahab as their model for cultural and political engagement (see 1 Kings 17). But like other biblical Old Testament prophets serving before the Jewish exile to Babylon, Elijah was serving as God's covenant prosecutor in calling Ahab back from his backslidden state. Elijah was called to minister in that manner because Israel was supposed to function under God's law as a theocracy. Attempting to employ that mode of ministry in a postmodern, humanistic context (like most of North America and Europe) will only marginalize and relegate you to just preaching to the choir!

The present Evangelical (Roman) method makes an initial contact with the surrounding community by presenting the Gospel and attempting to get folks to make a decision for Christ *before* they welcome them into their community. Instead, we need to mimic the Celtic saints of old who evangelized people groups by first having their community of faith embrace the pagan community around them. This effectively led to opportunities to present the Gospel and lead folks to make decisions for Christ. In other words, we need to send believers into the community before the community will want to come into our churches! We have to go from church-centric to community-centric. We have to train people for life in the marketplace—not just for church life. Pastors should be the chaplains of their community—not just the spiritual leader of those who attend their church on Sundays. We need to have favor with men before we can point them to God!

We need to understand what it means to put the Kingdom of God before our own local agendas and realize the long-lasting benefits from collaborative efforts among churches and leaders in the Body of Christ. God wants us to come to a place where we not only preach to our city but also love and serve our city or community. I believe that God will give the church influence commensurate to the amount of practical love displayed by her members.

Even Jesus healed the sick and fed the multitudes as part of His ministry. He served the people by meeting their physical needs before He attempted to connect them to the Father spiritually! We have to use the same strategy as the early church. They influenced the whole Roman empire by loving and serving one another and the heathen people around them. The church gained ascendancy in the Roman empire by giving human corpses left in garbage dumps a proper burial, utilizing bands of Christian mothers to nurse infants left to die in the streets, and taking care of the poor and the widows. When they gained political influence after Emperor Constantine's conversion in A.D. 313, they used it to disciple whole people groups.[1]

When the Kingdom Awakening begins to permeate an area, it will lead believers to go from individual Gospel-centric to Kingdom-centric—from merely preaching individual salvation to working to redeem whole communities and cities in accordance with Isaiah 61:1-4. Awakening the Church in a city like New York through infiltration and influence is not something a pastor or spiritual leader can attempt to do in his or her own strength. *"'Not by might, nor by power but by My Spirit,' says the Lord Almighty"* (Zech. 4:6 NIV). In John 5:18, Jesus said that He only did what He saw His Father doing, and Psalm 127 warns us that we can have "good" ideas, although they might not be "God" ideas.

I knew if I did not seek first His Kingdom and His way of doing things, I might end up building a lot of "good" things but laboring in vain. I definitely wanted to avoid fruitless activity! I also realized events alone would not transform my city, so I asked God to lead me and show me what and how He wanted His purposes accomplished. As a result, I resolved to pray and intercede daily for my city and its inhabitants.

From January 2, 1998, to the end of 2000, I began to experience such times of intense burden that I would need to alter my schedule and get alone with God until I had prayed the burden through. If I tried to speak with anyone other than God during these times, I found I was distracted and unable to focus because of the intense yearning on my heart to intercede and travail for my city. In the same way that Nehemiah and Jesus wept over Jerusalem, we are called to pour our souls out unto God for our specific region. It is only after we do this that God will grant us authority over that region and equip us to effectively advance His Kingdom in our sphere of influence.

One of the direct results of this intense travail was the birth of the City Covenant Coalition, a large network of interdenominational ministers in the New York City region who began to work together for the common good of the city. The City Action Coalition was birthed from there, which is a multicultural, clergy-led organization that is standing against unbiblical principles trying to permeate our society—like same-sex marriage. (As of the writing of this book, we have had great victories in defeating same-sex marriage in New York state and New Jersey in December 2009!) God has given us a common goal to educate the Body of Christ so that together we can apply biblical principles to public policy and infiltrate all areas of society for God's Kingdom. Only by partnering with other members of the Christian community can we truly begin to see His Kingdom come and His will be done on the earth as it is in Heaven.

My prayer is that as you read what we have walked through and learned in attempting to unite the Body of Christ here in our city, you will gain insights as to what God would have you do to bring His Kingdom influence to your city. First Corinthians 12 explains how God intends for the Body of Christ to function. *"The body is a unit, though it is made up of many parts,"* and all parts are of equal importance so there is to be no division or jealousy among us (1 Cor. 12:12 NIV). We must learn to partner together for the good of the whole:

> ...*prepare God's people for works of service so that the Body of Christ may be built up until we reach unity in the faith and in the knowledge of the Son of God and become mature, attaining to the whole measure of the fullness of Christ* (Ephesians 4:13 NIV).

Endnote

1. For more reference material on all this, read *How the Irish Saved Civilization* by Cahill, *Why You Think the Way You Do* by Glen S. Sunshine, *The Celtic Way of Evangelism* by George Hunter III, and *The Urban Christian* by Ray Baake.

CHAPTER 1

PARTNERING IN THE KINGDOM

I started ministering in the Sunset Park section of Brooklyn, New York, in 1980. At the time, this community was ridden with gang violence, abandoned buildings, drug addiction, and poverty. Actually, New York City as a whole was not politically or financially healthy, having requested a federal government bailout to prevent financial bankruptcy! There were many communities like ours during this time that were existing in a day-to-day atmosphere of poverty and fear.

I was a typical, zealous new minister who thought that my great preaching was going to result in a powerful revival in our city with multitudes of people flocking to our new church. However, after about five years, I entered into a time of great trial and discovered that the foundation of my family and my ministry was on shaky ground. I almost lost both! It was during this intense season of trying to survive in the midst of great spiritual warfare that I realized how much I needed to partner with other pastors and churches if I was going to succeed in my mission to transform New York City.

As I sought to help alleviate the causes of destructive influences in our community, I decided to see if I could partner with the local Evangelical church organization and work with pastors and programs already in existence. What I discovered, though, was that the Evangelical church as a whole didn't seem to have much in the way of unity. As a result, very little was being accomplished as far as cultural change was concerned. Consequently, in 1991 I began a season of intense personal prayer, which resulted in a call for an "All-City Prayer." I had a 12-member leadership team made up of senior pastors of some of the largest churches in our tri-state region who came together to pray and fast for our city.

It was during this intense season of trying to survive in the midst of great spiritual warfare that I realized how much I needed to partner with other pastors and churches if I was going to succeed in my mission to transform New York City.

This became a catalyst for a significant united prayer effort in New York City among churches that were previously not connected together. Leaders and members from about 60 churches came together several times, with one meeting bringing together almost 3,000 people!

After conducting these meetings for two years, I was introduced to Mac Pier, the New York director of Concerts of Prayer International, who told me that he was already heading up a united citywide prayer effort. COPI involved Evangelical churches under the national leadership of David Bryant. At that point, I had to make a decision. I was preaching unity in the Body of Christ as the greatest need for revival, but now I realized that we had two separate prayer movements in our region.

I believed the correct thing to do was to defer to COPI because they started before us.

As a result of my burgeoning relationship with Mac Pier and my decision to partner with the existing organization, I became a bridge between some of the major charismatic churches in our city and COPI. I eventually became one of the founding trustees of Concerts of Prayer Greater New York. I believe that because of our "All City Prayer" events, New York was spared the violence of the riots that took place after the police beating of Rodney King. Not only that, but we also saw a significant drop in the crime rate as we joined together to intercede and pray over our city. The prayer movement spearheaded by COPGNY is still going strong, and today New York City has been deemed the safest city in America among those with a population of over one million people.

> **I believe that because we came together in prayer, New York was spared the violence of the Rodney King-inspired race riots.**

Wash the Feet of Ministers

During the course of my citywide ministry, I have learned an important axiom: "The person or organization who serves, leads." In other words, those who provide an indispensable service to a person, organization, or community will be respected and needed. For example, in 1989, I organized a large collection of religious, political, and community leaders in Sunset Park who banded together to close a pornographic store near a grammar school, which of course benefited all the families in the entire community and gave the churches favor with many of the residents.

Those who provide an indispensable service to a person, organization, or community will be respected and needed.

Dr. Mac Pier and the Concerts of Prayer of Greater New York has expanded so that it now networks hundreds of churches and has implemented such community-minded initiatives as world AIDS outreaches to children in partnership with World Vision International, powerful Gatekeeper training events, and Leadership Summits featuring such influential speakers as Bill Hybels and the leadership of Willow Creek Church.

In the late 1990s, the Lord also led me to bring together a multi-ethnic group of pastors in New York City for a series of Unity Communion Services, which have involved more than 50 Caucasian, Asian, and Hispanic pastors. To demonstrate reconciliation and the unity in New York City, we converged on an all-black community to partake of communion together with African American pastors and their congregants. These Unity Communion Services and multi-ethnic events like this have had a profound impact on breaking down racially motivated divisions in our city. For example, many of the pastors involved in these initiatives have continued to serve together in our city for almost twenty years and become a model for ethnic harmony that has smashed the stereotypes of racial division! (One example is City Covenant Coalition, which was started in 1999 and was founded by myself and one of the leading African American Pastors in New York City, Bishop Roderick Caesar, Jr.)

Walls between key Black, Hispanic, and Caucasian leaders have been broken down and it has helped bring a greater sense of Christian love that has permeated our congregations and even impacted those in the political arena who didn't think ethnic unity was possible and plausible. The catalyst for these communion services was a series of events I initiated with Dr. John Perkins and other city leaders entitled "Building Bridges: Racial Reconciliation Retreat and Meetings." We assembled 20 of the top African American and Caucasian leaders in New York City and met together in a small Manhattan apartment to hash out differences, break down ethnic barriers, and bring racial healing to the Body of Christ. A few of the African American leaders I met with in that small Manhattan apartment have since become an integral part of the citywide Christ Covenant Coalition (formerly City Covenant Coalition). This coalition branched out to include numerous social and political outreaches and has included hundreds of church and marketplace leaders in New York City who are committed to seeing our city transformed by the Kingdom of God.

We have come a long way and have had to overcome other major obstacles in partnering together to bring unity to our city. Years ago, when pastors began to minister to and demonstrate a concern for ministries and congregations other than their own, they were met with suspicion and distrust. I witnessed this first-hand when one of the pastors who attended the support group for clergy I started suddenly stopped, saying he had an issue with me. When I met with him, he looked me straight in the eyes and asked me what my agenda was. I purposefully looked straight back into his eyes and told him sincerely that my "agenda" was him and that my call was to wash the feet of the pastors in our community. I explained that I was called to advance the Kingdom of God, not to build my own empire!

I had learned a valuable lesson a few years earlier when I was about to plant two churches in our area. The Lord clearly spoke to me, saying that if I truly wanted to impact my city for Him, I was to refocus my energy into blessing the other leaders of the Body of Christ that He already had in place there. From that point on, I began to spend anywhere from 50 to 80 percent of my time ministering to other pastors and building up existing local churches.

Our church even began to send "Kingdom Offerings" to financially bless various local congregations in our region; We also helped pay the salary of a senior pastor for several weeks when one local church was struggling financially; and one month, we even paid the home mortgage for a local pastor who couldn't pay his bills! This brought incredible unity and trust between pastors that released the blessing of God in our midst, and I don't believe it is a coincidence that many of those pastors in "covenant" together also received the financial provision to acquire their own church buildings before long. Since property in the NYC region is very expensive, many local churches rent space from public schools or from other congregations, so this was truly a great blessing for the relatively new nondenominational churches we were working with.

The Lord clearly spoke to me, saying that if I truly wanted to impact my city for Him, I was to refocus my energy into blessing the other leaders of the Body of Christ that He already had in place there.

Often leaders are only concerned with their own local church, which stifles the cooperation and unity of the Body of Christ and robs her of universality and power. According to the apostle Paul, there may be many congregations, but there should only be one Body of Christ (see 1 Cor. 12). We cannot function cohesively unless we are motivated by the overarching theme of bringing the King-dom of God to earth.

> The church does not establish the parameters of God's reign; the parameters of God's reign define the role of the church. The church has not always gotten this sequence right.[1]

Seek Out the Apostolic Leaders

Before I started City Covenant Coalition, I spent a year gathering apostolic leaders all the way from Connecticut to New Jersey. An apostolic leader is a person with significant influence in a region, city, or nation who is sent out by God as His ambassador or representative. Second Corinthians 10:13-16 speaks of the ecclesial sphere of authority given to bishops and apostles that must be respected. Although we are all given authority over our own lives and in our spheres of influence, we cannot move with authority in a certain realm of society if we have not been ordained by God for that specific realm or region. Thus, we must be skilled at coalition or team building if we are going to success-fully reach various regions for the Gospel.

We must always remember that this is mainly a spiritual bat-tle and can only be fought if we have the keys from Heaven and use our God-given authority to serve a specific region. We must be covered spiritually so that we aren't suddenly waylaid simply because we haven't moved through the hierarchical structure that God designed for victory in these spiritual realms, which will manifest in the natural as a region or realm of society.

To bypass apostolic leaders without receiving their partner-ship or blessing means that our success may be greatly limited and we might even fail in our efforts. God will not work against or without those to whom He has given legal rights and authority.

We see this principle in Deuteronomy 2:5 and 2:9 when God warned Israel not to meddle with or go to war against the children of Esau in Mount Seir or the Moabites because He already granted them the legal right to that land as their inheritance.

> **To bypass apostolic leaders without receiving their partnership or blessing means that our success may be greatly limited and we might even fail in our efforts.**

The best advice I can give to a new pastor, to those involved in planting a church, and even to those wishing to start a new business or organization in their region, is to first seek out and get to know those with an apostolic calling over that region. Visit some of the churches, meet the pastors, and join a local ministerial fellowship. Align yourself with, be coached by, receive blessing from, and network with apostolic leaders, because they have significant influence in their region as representatives of the Kingdom. This allows you and the existing congregations and ministries in the community an opportunity to represent the Kingdom of God in your city, community, or town. In cases where apostolic leaders are either not present or not readily available to align with you, find an apostolic leader in a nearby city or region to coach you and endorse you until such time as appropriate apostolic leadership manifests itself in your city.

With respect to the apostolic rule in missions, our organization will not even plant a church in another country that already has a strong church presence because we believe that God has assigned bishops and apostolic leaders within that sphere of authority. I don't even allow local church pastors in other countries to come under my covering. I always defer to the apostolic leaders in their region. I go to other nations to serve their leaders, not to take influence and tithe money home with me.

Love Your City

Now we come to "the greatest of these." We cannot claim an area for God without truly loving it. Usually, the people and places that we find we have an emotional connection with and a heartfelt divine love for are those God has called us to and given us responsibility over. To the surprise of many, I love New York City, and I would live here even if I did not need to because of my pastorate. I love the multi-ethnic milieu, especially the many quality ethnic restaurants located within walking distance of my house! I count myself blessed that I am privileged to minister in perhaps the most influential city in the history of the world.

For the first time in history, more than 50 percent of the world's population now lives in cities, so those of us in megacities like New York don't have to travel to reach the nations. The nations have come to us! Erwin Raphael McManus said:

> For years the bulk of American Christians who were committed to missions could only participate through giving and praying. Today, the call to cross-cultural ministry doesn't require going; it just requires staying with a purpose.[2]

We must begin to understand that the city we serve is also a gift to the church; it's not just that the church is a gift to the city. Each city has a redemptive gift, and those who tap into and harness it with the power of the Gospel are able to minister to the maximum number of people in their community. A redemptive gift is a unique vocation or ability given by God to an individual, organization, or city to serve humanity. Some cities, like Rome, have served historically as a model for organization and societal order. The city of Athens is a model for philosophy and wisdom. Because of Wall Street and the United Nations, New York City has served the world primarily as its financial and leadership hub.

A redemptive gift is a unique vocation or ability given by God to an individual, organization, or city to serve humanity.

Having this mind-set has given me the theological permission to work closely with all political and community leaders who are committed to our city's success whether or not they are Christian. For example, a few days after 9/11, I went to the local police precinct and gave all the officers books that dealt with pain and loss. I also set up a borough-wide strategy that provided the precincts with a list of all the local churches that offered grief counseling. Many of us worked 18-hour days with various initiatives, including outreaches to the NYPD and our communities for the six months following September 11, 2001. Looking back, the church was ready to collaborate and accomplish these major initiatives because of the unity we had already practiced for many years!

As a result, the commanding police officer in my community asked me to be a part of a community-wide crisis management team that discusses the needs of the community and ways we can safeguard against terrorism. To this day, political, community, and law enforcement officials and leaders call on me for advice, help, mediation, prayer, and the use of our facilities for various functions or community meetings. Because the community knows of our compassionate outreach to at-risk children and youth, and the numerous ways we have utilized strategic initiatives to alleviate common problems, we have earned the right to speak prophetically to the powers that be with regard to same-sex marriage and other relevant moral issues affecting our society.

To Be Effective, Be Aware

I learned a long time ago that a seminary education that only deals with biblical hermeneutics (interpretation) is not enough to prepare a person for ministry in the Kingdom. To be effective, we need to be aware of social issues, concerns, and events in our culture, community, and world. After events such as 9/11, Hurricane Katrina, the tsunami of December 2004, the economic collapse of global markets, and the earthquake in Haiti, communicators and leaders need to have the Bible in one hand and the newspaper in the other. Current issues should be addressed with a biblical response or explanation from the pulpit as well as through community outreaches. Leaders who can't provide biblical answers for such events are ill-equipped for high-level regional leadership in such a complex world.

> **Current issues should be addressed with a biblical response or explanation from the pulpit as well as through community outreaches.**

Christians aspiring to be effective cultural influencers need to read current events with a biblical lens so that both the challenges and solutions are framed in their minds. Then the Kingdom of God will be effectively reflected through them in their various realms of influence. We should consistently ask for statistics from the police and health department as well as from local political leaders to keep us well informed on the ever-changing dynamics of our cities and communities. We are called to serve, bless, and befriend the key business, community, and civic leaders of our area so we can more effectively position the Gospel and the Church to be salt and light.

As a member of my local community board for several years, I was regularly briefed as to the economic, political, and sociological trends of importance to us as local regional representatives. To be effective, we must be aware of what is going on in the world around us and be ready to help implement biblically based principles to any situation as it arises. Paul told young Timothy:

> *Herald and preach the Word!* **Keep your sense of urgency** *[stand by, be at hand and ready], whether the opportunity seems to be favorable or unfavorable. [Whether it is convenient or inconvenient, whether it is welcome or unwelcome, you as preacher of the Word are to show people in what way their lives are wrong.] And convince them, rebuking and correcting, warning and urging and encouraging them, being unflagging and inexhaustible in patience and teaching* (2 Timothy 4:2 AMP).

Be Offense-Free

Love includes a principle that is not always easy for us to follow: we must learn to be "thick skinned." To be a leader means that we will receive criticism, whether constructive or not, and we will always have people oppose us, no matter how great of a leader we may be. We must learn the nature of offense-free relationships or we will never survive in this world we are called to influence for His Kingdom. I have found that because many leaders lack organizational ability or have overloaded schedules and numerous congregational emergencies, it is hard for them to stay connected to other pastors and consistently commit to anything outside of their church.

Unfortunately, some leaders may also have a spirit of competition and theological insecurity. Years ago, a few pastors in our area stopped attending our local community meeting because some of the other members prayed for the sick in a way that offended them. By doing this, they cut off their only means of peer support. Consequently, most of those leaders didn't survive the high demands of ministry required in a New York City pastorate.

I have learned to continually move on with what the Lord is directing me and not hold any grudges. I understand that it takes perseverance to work with diverse groups and that quality relationships don't just happen—they require hard work. We have to be able to develop tough skin, as we will always find various leaders who will either be wavering in their commitments or subtly oppose us in our community efforts. My motto is, "Have thick skin but a soft heart!"

My motto is, "Have thick skin but a soft heart!"

However, confrontation may still be necessary to really allow the relationship to continue to be effective. When it comes to confrontation, I endeavor to follow the procedure Jesus gave in Matthew 18:15-17. If people I am in relationship with say or do something that negatively affects the way I feel toward them or impedes my ability to work with them, I immediately confront them in love, thereby not allowing the enemy a foothold in our relationship. The devil has only one plan for the Body of Christ, and that is to bring division. If the air is clear and there is ample communication between key leadership, then there is no room for schisms and the enemy will fail in his attempt to divide and conquer.

To truly build lasting and effective relationships within the Body of Christ, we need to understand that all meaningful relationships experience three distinct stages. First there is the *honeymoon* stage when you first meet a person and only notice his or her strongest qualities and giftings. Within a few weeks this person may actually become one of your closest friends. But before you entrust your secrets and heart to him or her, allow your relationship to go through stage two, the *disillusionment* stage. As you get to know this person more intimately, you will begin to notice his or her quirks and character flaws. The most mature people are those who plow through the disillusionment stage until they reach the third stage—*reality*. This is when you view the person the way he or she really is and the way God sees him or her. Only the emotionally mature, those secure in who they are in Christ and who are committed to covenant, will make it to the *reality* stage. The more mature you are, the less you put folks on a pedestal, thus the less impact the second and third stages will have on your relationship.

I recently had an experience where I walked through these stages with a leader I greatly admired. I was thrilled when I was first introduced to him and was greatly impressed with his humility and willingness to work closely together with us. It was only a matter of a few months, however, before my respect for this person began to be tested because of his lack of follow-through concerning coalition plans and meetings. I decided to stick it out and have since learned to overlook some of his administration foibles because I see his intent and heart commitment. This person has become an integral part of one of my organizations, and I believe we can produce great fruit together for the Kingdom!

This would never have happened had I decided to opt out during the disillusionment stage of our relationship.

Honor Those Who Have Gone Before

One of the highlights of my life was in the year 2000 when the City Covenant Coalition honored 12 apostolic leaders who had faithfully served as pastors in the New York City region for 20 years or more. Multi-denominational, multi-ethnic leaders stood together on a platform to receive honor and appreciation from hundreds of other leaders and peers for their many years of service to our city. The most touching moment was when one of these leaders openly wept before us, sharing that it was the first time he had ever been affirmed in such a way by his ministerial colleagues. It was also the first time any of us had witnessed our community of faith coming together to honor our spiritual heroes. Events like this are vitally important if we want to build unity and alter the destiny of a city!

The apostle Paul took the time in his epistles to honor those who had faithfully labored in the Lord, and he commanded the churches to highly esteem those who labored in the Gospel.[3] As the Body of Christ, we must show our appreciation for the positive influence Christian leadership has had on our own lives and on the lives of those in our community and nation.

As the Body of Christ, we must show our appreciation for the positive influence Christian leadership has had on our own lives and in the lives of those on our community and nation.

When City Covenant Coalition honored the spiritual fathers of our city, one of the criteria was that they had served at least 20 years in the pastorate. It has personally taken me almost 10 years to develop the kind of network needed to have an effective outreach in our community and to develop deeply rooted relationships with the local community board, public schools, city police departments, elected officials, and key business and community leaders. The networking in our local community is now so extensive that it feels like one big happy family working together for the good of thousands of area residents. This is how the Body of Christ is supposed to function here on the earth and is really the only effective way to fulfill the great commission! To accomplish this, we must become effective team builders.

Effective Team Building

In my present work as the presiding bishop of Christ Covenant Coalition, I operate with a very diversified leadership team, and each member has expertise in a specific realm or area. It is exciting to come together with a team that is in covenant with one another, and that allows each of us to utilize our specific gifts to empower pastors and marketplace leaders and effectively promote God's Kingdom in our region. Although being a minister can sometimes make us feel that we must always have the answers, I have learned to surround myself with the leaders that God has already equipped to be experts, and call on them to meet the needs of the people and the community. I know God will provide what is needed, just as He provided skilled workmen to build the Tabernacle in the wilderness under Moses' direction (see Exod. 31:1-10).

I have learned how to match qualified network leaders to the needs of people. For example, when one of the pastors was involved with planting a new church, I referred him to one of our leaders who has successfully planted a number of churches. When another leader needed financial advice, I referred him to one of our marketplace financial advisors. One of the most powerful examples of this is when I was able to assemble a team and furnish legal advice, counseling, and pastoral care for a church when the pastor was unable to function properly due to a tragedy in his family.

Perhaps the most important element with regard to developing effective and fruitful partnerships in the Kingdom is integrity, which in turn allows trust to flow and produces synergy and power. *Trust* is the key element that determines how far we can go with our fellow laborers in the advancement of the Kingdom. Relationships precede ministry, and trust precedes meaningful relationships. One of the reasons some of us have had a high success rate with regard to developing and maintaining effective coalitions in our region is because we endeavor to disarm insecurities and fears among leaders by building an atmosphere of covenant and trust.

> **Perhaps the most important element with regard to developing effective and fruitful partnerships in the Kingdom is integrity, which in turn allows trust to flow and produces synergy and power.**

I believe trust comes from:

1. *Upholding proper protocol and avoiding "sheep stealing."* When you are committed to one another's success, then you can wholeheartedly encourage members and

leaders of local churches even when you are preaching in their service. A pastor who had a church just four short blocks away from mine had me take his place when he went on vacation and preach for him without worrying that he would lose members of his church to our congregation. When I was preaching in his church, I celebrated his leadership and their vision! Proper protocol also includes receiving proper clearance before counseling people overseen by another leader. The reason I have so much trust among the leaders in my city is because I laid out boundaries that controlled and guided my relationships with their churches and congregations so we can work together without fear.

2. *Avoiding listening to only one side of the story.* Sometimes leaders may have problems with one another and I am called in to act as a mediator and try to bring reconciliation. I learned a long time ago that I need to hear both sides of a story in order to have the proper context to make wise decisions. Taking the time to truly discern all the facts in any situation allows everyone to trust that the outcome will be godly motivated.

3. *Avoiding the use of citywide meetings to fulfill personally motivated ambitions, such as collecting contact information as a way of soliciting financial support and / or membership.* This is tragic and extremely detrimental to building effective teams. All such citywide events should be for the purpose of expanding the Kingdom of God and unifying the Body of Christ in the community, not raising the profile of an individual pastor, minister, or church.

To avoid potential problems like these, we will not admit a leader as a member of Christ Covenant Coalition unless he or she is a bishop, senior pastor, or head of a ministry or business. We do not want to be in a position in which we teach something different than what the local church pastor or church believes, thus becoming the cause of a schism in their church. We would much rather deal with the senior leaders so we can maintain a safe environment for all involved and establish relationships based on a foundation of trust and integrity.

Building Strong Local Churches Increases Kingdom Influence

Up until a few years ago, I was probably the only minister in our region who was simultaneously overseeing a substantial local church and a large, influential network of clergy and churches. Doing both is difficult, but I learned a long time ago that having a strong local church model leveraged my influence with our network and other extra-local activities. I counsel other pastors that they should never compromise their local church for citywide events. As a rule of thumb, I advise pastors to never get involved in an event that will hurt or distract them from building an effective local model. The local model is their primary financial base for ministry and the motivation for their participation in citywide functions. Thus, if their church is hurting or not functioning properly, they cannot be effective in reaching out to their community.

Years ago, I was part of a network of churches that began to subtly put down the ministry of a pastor by implying that his or her main job was to raise up elders as quickly as possible to take over the leadership of the church. Then he was to resign from the pastorate and trans-locally minister to other pastors and churches. The biblical ideal, however, is to have the executive (apostolic) pastor train leaders so that he can travel and minister extensively to other pastors and other congregations while still remaining the overseer of the local church. The apostle Paul felt this was so important an issue that he dedicated several letters to instructing pastors under his leadership how to effectively deal with the qualifications and duties of the pastorate and their leadership team.[4]

Jesus spoke about the *"keys of the Kingdom"* in the context of building the church in Matthew 16:18-19. I believe part of what Jesus was speaking about in this passage was that senior leaders of apostolic churches have great authority to tear down satan's Kingdom in their community. Through the years, I have had numerous people tell me that I should resign my pastorate and give myself over to totally serving the Body of Christ in my region. I have never followed that advice because I believe that the local church is the key to fulfilling the purposes of God on the earth and to resign would be giving away too much influence and credibility (although at some point I may be forced to be less involved in the day-to-day affairs).

For example, during any given week, because of the influence of our congregation, I may have a meeting with local educators as we attempt to start a charter school. I may be asked to visit a city councilperson who needs advice, or called upon to help a high-ranking person in the police department find somebody who can mediate a problem between two ethnic groups or religious sects. I may be asked to offer the invocation and speak at a special event honoring the fallen heroes of 9/11, or meet with one of the leaders of a health insurance company who wants to partner with our children's charity. I might discuss plans with a bank manager who wants to do a regional financial management seminar for local pastors and church members. I could also be asked to facilitate a city-wide ecumenical meeting hosted by a political leader who is trying to bring racial and religious understanding to our community.

I take great joy in the fact that I have two congregations— the church world and the marketplace. Just as many high-level secular marketplace leaders consider me their pastor or spiritual leader as do pastors in our organization and congregation. My wife has been featured numerous times in mainstream secular media like *Access Hollywood* and the *New York Daily News*. We regularly meet with pro athletes and businesspeople, because those called to reflect the Kingdom of God on earth should feel just as comfortable with non-Christians as with Christians.

I was once called upon to minister to a high-level investment banker who managed operations in ten nations. After speaking with me, she told her friend that I sounded more like a corporate business leader than a bishop! Once you are converted to the Kingdom message, you truly see the whole world as your parish and can effectively relate to anyone God sends you to! Partnering for the advancement of the Kingdom of God becomes easy when you see the whole world as your call.

Think on This

We need to understand what it means to put the Kingdom of God before our own local agendas and realize the long-lasting benefits from collaborative efforts among churches and leaders in the Body of Christ. God wants us to come to a place where we not only preach to our city but also love and serve our city or community. I believe that God will give the church influence commensurate to the amount of practical love displayed by her members.

Think on the following questions:

1. What creative ways can you expand the influence of the Kingdom of God by networking with other key people in your realm of influence?

2. What can you and your organization do to honor the faithful spiritual leaders in your community?

3. How can you begin to develop relational trust among the key churches and community leaders in your area?

ISLAM territorial / Kingdom. RELATIONAL

Before reading further, I would suggest that if understanding the church's role in influencing culture is a new concept for you, first read Appendix A. How the Church impacts the culture and functions within the Kingdom of God is a critical issue. You may also want to read my first book on this topic, *Kingdom Revolution*.

We need to understand what it means to put the Kingdom of God before our own local agendas and realize the long-lasting benefits from collaborative efforts among churches and leaders in the Body of Christ.

Then, as you go through the material in this book, begin to journal ways God reveals to you that will open up new relationships in and around your community and city to further His Kingdom principles in your area of influence.

Endnotes

1. Craig Van Gelder, *The Essence of the Church: A Community Created by the Spirit* (Grand Rapids, Michigan: Baker Books, 2000), 87.

2. Erwin Raphael McManus, *An Unstoppable Force: Daring to Become the Church God Had in Mind* (Loveland, Colorado: Group Publishing, 2001), 45.

3. Read First Thessalonians 5:12-13, Romans 16:3-16, Second Corinthians 8:18, and Philippians 2:19-22.

4. Read First Timothy, Second Timothy, and Titus, known as the pastoral letters.

Chapter 2

Partnering and Ethnicity

After these things I looked, and behold, a great multitude which no one could count, from every nation and all tribes and peoples and tongues, standing before the throne and before the Lamb, clothed in white robes, and palm branches were in their hands (Revelation 7:9 NASB).

I remember the day my friends first found out that my mother, Miriam, was Puerto Rican instead of Italian. They started making fun of me, dancing wildly, and calling my mother "Miriam Makeba," mimicking the then-famous female singer. From that time on, I was identified as a "spic" and other words that I could never put in this book.

Instead of feeling sorry for myself or sulking, I would just give it right back to them and make fun of their parents and their own particular ethnic background.

In trying to deal with the ethnic differences that apparently determined how I was going to be treated by my peers, I made sure that I excelled in sports, physically confronted some of my antagonists, and became a master at witty verbal comebacks. It didn't take long before the neighborhood bullies hesitated to make fun of me because they knew the penalty they would pay. By the time I was in the seventh grade, I was a prolific athlete, an accomplished street fighter, and generally feared and respected by most of the kids in the neighborhood. Although most of our jostling was done in fun, it revealed a deeper hidden prejudice that the children in this Caucasian neighborhood had picked up from their parents.

Most of my friends reflected the racism of their parents, with many of my teenage peers openly expressing their hatred of black people. I still don't know why, but I never acquiesced to their racist positions and even had numerous arguments with family and friends because I felt that black people were no different, no better and no worse than Caucasian people. As a professional musician, I played in clubs with all-black bands and jammed with black musicians who became some of my closest friends.

I remember one sad day when I was about 18 years old—I saw an enraged mob of about 20 white teens chasing a terrified black teen. I grabbed him right before the gang of whites caught up with him, put him behind my back, and hoped my reputation as a street fighter would be enough to ward them off. In spite of my reputation, they continued to try to punch and grab him, accusing him of robbing one of the local neighborhood kids. I tried to protect him, but there were simply too many of them and I was outnumbered. When I saw that I could no longer protect him, I got in front of him in a way that enabled him to escape with a slight head start before the enraged group took up the chase again. To this day I don't know what happened to that kid, but I saw the effect of racial prejudice up close and personal.

Growing up in New York City in the 1970s, I also witnessed the effect of racial unrest as every ethnic group formed their own gang. The Italians had the "Golden Guineas," the blacks had a gang called the "Spades," and the Spanish had the "Young Lords" as well as a second ferocious gang called the "Savage Skulls." I befriended a fellow freshman at the beginning of my high school career and would regularly walk ten blocks to the subway station with him. One day, a group of about 12 Hispanic kids walked past us, violently pushing my friend out of the way. I challenged the person who pushed him, not aware of the fact that he was connecting to this group as the leader of the Savage Skulls. The kid I was protecting ran away and left me alone to face the group, even though he was a self-described expert in karate. I decided the easiest way to get out of that mess would be to stand there and take their beating. Thank God, the leader only kicked me in the face and gave me a black eye and then left me alone.

I told some of my senior friends what had happened, and both the Italian and the black gang leaders pledged to combine their two gangs to fight all the Hispanic gangs the next day on my behalf. That night I asked myself if this was really what I wanted to happen. I knew that if I didn't swallow my pride, the episode would escalate into a full-blown race riot that would result in numerous injuries and deaths. The next day, I walked to the headquarters of the Savage Skulls by myself and called off the fight between the gangs. The leader of the Savage Skulls apologized to me for what he had done, explaining he was in a bad mood because he had just had a fight with his girlfriend. Though these memories are somewhat painful to look back on, I realize that much of my passion to see Revelation 7:9 manifest in my lifetime has been fueled by my own personal experiences.

Roots of Our Separation

I want to take a look at the underlying issues that have caused ethnic separation in our communities and even in our churches. I have found that it primarily has to do with the inherent human desire to build with others of the same language, beliefs, and economic systems. One reason American churches are alike in ethnicity is because most communities are made up of homogeneous ethnic pockets. Thus, a congregation in a Hispanic community reflects this demographic. Of course, language presents obvious barriers, especially with first-generation immigrants.

> **One reason American churches are alike in ethnicity is because most communities are made up of homogeneous ethnic pockets.**

However, it must also be stated that there are numerous congregations in multicultural communities that believe a multi-ethnic church will work against the church growth principle of homogeneity, so they purposefully cater to a one-dimensional demographic. Even so-called multi-ethnic churches don't always solve the challenges of race relations either. Blacks, whites, Asians, and Hispanics may assemble together for Sunday services but separately congregate for church dinners, picnics, and fellowships.

When we look back at our church roots, we realize that it was the pagans in Greco-Roman culture that gave believers the name

Christians because the church at Antioch constructed a multi-ethnic leadership team (see Acts 11:26; 13:1). Although the city of Antioch erected walls that separated the various ethnic groups, those in the congregation scaled the walls and attended the city church together because believers in the Messiah were no longer exclusively Jewish. In Acts 2:5-41, the church became multilingual. In Acts 11:19-26, the church became multi-ethnic and multicultural. It is interesting that the world named believers in Christ *Christians* over 2,000 years ago because of their unity, but today we are called hypocrites because of our division!

No Greater Model of Love

Because America is mostly divided in ethnicity in the areas of education and communities, congregations that reflect the ethnicity of the Kingdom are a tremendous witness of the power of the Gospel to redeem and reconcile the world back to the Father! John 17:21-23 teaches us that the world will believe Jesus was sent by the Father *only* when the church is united.

> **Because America is mostly divided in ethnicity in the areas of education and communities, congregations that reflect the ethnicity of the Kingdom are a tremendous witness of the power of the Gospel to redeem and reconcile the world back to the Father!**

In 1984, my wife Joyce and I founded a church in a multi-ethnic community. Today we are a thriving urban church of about

40 different nationalities with almost ten different spoken languages. At one point, our Children of the City organization had an Asian office manager, the grant writer was from Trinidad, the executive director was of Arab and Polish descent, and the counselors were Jamaican, Hispanic, Italian, and Puerto Rican. We didn't try to do this; it was simply a reflection of the ethos of our congregation in which our Christianity transcended the walls of ethnicity, as we believed we are all made from one blood (see Acts 17:26). Historically, our church leadership has included a multi-ethnic team made up of African American, Hispanic, Irish, Italian, English, and Norwegian men and women.

However, I remember a meeting I had with a high-level ethnic church leader who was trying to discourage me from having a large multi-ethnic rally in New York City. He believed that a large body of one particular ethnic group would have more political clout than an ethnically diverse advocacy group. He told me, "Blacks should stick together and have their own rallies; whites should stick together and have their own events, and Hispanics should do the same." I believe he said this because of the way the media portrays and highlights all issues related to race relations, and because our culture is wired to respond more quickly to issues if they are connected to ethnicity or race relations. In essence, his view was that coalition building is best done by members of one's own ethnicity. My response to him was that even though it may have worked better politically to work separately, working together did fit the biblical model of Revelation 7:9 and fulfill the call of Jesus that we reflect Heaven and God's Kingdom on the earth (see Luke 11:2).

Bridge Building

I have been working as what I call a bridge builder for almost two decades in New York City. In the 1990s, the Lord impressed upon my heart to ask some of the top African American and Caucasian church leaders to come to a "Building Bridges Racial Reconciliation Meeting." We purposely crammed 25 leaders into a small Manhattan apartment so we would be forced to look into each other's eyes! The meeting did not seem to be going anywhere until one of the African American leaders spoke up and said, "I can't trust a white man as far as I can throw him!" That burst of honesty blew the whole meeting wide open and led the way for a time of intense but productive dialogue. It was followed up with a 48-hour "Building Bridges Racial Reconciliation Retreat" and four years of "Unity Communion" services.

As a result of these initial steps toward racial reconciliation, I galvanized a group of Caucasian, Hispanic, and Asian pastors to celebrate Communion together in an African American church in Bedford Stuyvesant, Brooklyn. Many of the blacks in the neighborhood thought the church was being raided by the FBI when they saw white men dressed in suits walking into the church! When we told them we wanted to celebrate Communion with them, not only the congregation but the entire neighborhood was positively impacted. We continued to fellowship together, and it has produced deep, long-lasting covenantal friendships among key leaders in our city. Many of these same leaders now serve on the executive board of the various networks I oversee in the New York region.

I also serve on the board of a nonprofit community-based organization called CURE (Community Understanding for Racial and Ethnic Equality). For years we have regularly met with various ethnic and religious leaders for the purpose of dialogue, understanding, and cross-pollination. We have held numerous forums attended by public officials as well as local political and business leaders. At a number of these forums, I have told those in attendance that I have heard the N-word more when among blacks than among whites and that we have the continual challenge of "black-on-black" and "white-on-white" crime. I added that I had noticed many Latinos don't associate with Hispanics of other nationalities and that many ethnic Asians don't even get along together. I rarely see Mexicans and Cubans fellowship with Puerto Ricans and Dominicans in my neighborhood, and in my travels I have also noticed how Chinese and Koreans don't usually mingle.

I told my audiences that the real problem transcends race because it is spelled S-I-N. Until all ethnic groups come to the cross, there will never be any lasting peace. Believe it or not, I have always received a very favorable response from these mostly non-Christian audiences! Even non-Christians resonate with the idea that there is something inside all of us that tempts us to act unjustly toward our fellow brothers and sisters of this world.

> **I told my audiences that the real problem transcends race because it is spelled S-I-N.**

I believe the only cure for ethnic or economic division is for people to experience the unconditional love of God and witness the example of the cross of Christ. Jesus reconciled the world back to Himself, thus displaying a love so vast and deep that it has never been nor ever will be witnessed again by our natural eyes. In Christ *alone* there is neither black nor white, slave or free, rich or poor, male or female. We are all one in Christ Jesus! My pastor always used to say, "The ground is level at the cross!" And Proverbs 22:2 states, *"The rich and poor meet together; the Lord is the Maker of them all."*

Salad Bowl or Melting Pot?

A look at Genesis 10–11 tells us that God divided the nations after the flood. He desires diversity in the human race in the same way an artist utilizes different colors in a painting. God is not color blind. He made black men black, white men white, and so on. Because of this, black is beautiful, but so is white, yellow, brown, etc. So, the Christian perspective must include an understanding that God made the universe with the purpose of having unity *within* diversity—one unified system in which diversity can flourish. Unity is not conformity; it is diversity with a common purpose or goal.

Unity is not conformity; it is diversity with a common purpose or goal.

Many African American and Hispanic church leaders have told me they espouse the *salad bowl* model of unity, in which all ethnic groups keep their particular cultures intact and relate together from that vantage point. They do not like the old American goal of creating a melting pot, because acculturation into "white America" would cause them to lose their voice and power. Thus, they feel they would be throwing out all advances made in the Civil Rights movement.

By reflecting on black U.S. history, this is an understandable approach. For centuries, all African Americans ever had were their communities, families, and churches. The church was the concentric power base that holistically developed communities, created credit unions, built housing, and aided parents in raising their children. The black church continues to be way ahead of its time as a model to all churches that are attempting to holistically transform culture. Their primary concern is to develop the next generation of black leadership. They know from experience that if their young people move away and assimilate into the majority culture, both the ground they have gained in racial reform and their voice to bring about further change would be lost. The new middle to upper class black leadership might then advocate the values of the majority culture and forget the people and communities they came from.

This is a complex problem that has no simple solutions outside of God's intervention. However, I would like to make a few observations regarding the salad bowl and melting pot approach to ethnicity in America that will give us insight as to the problems we face and the responsibilities we have as Christians to uphold Kingdom principles in the midst of racial diversity.

Mixed Veggies

Like a mixed salad that holds a diverse collection of vegetables, including tomatoes, lettuce, onions, mushrooms, avocados, cucumbers, etc., this view holds that America should be a collection of distinct ethnic groups that hold onto their cultural identities and nuances while living and serving together with other ethnic groups. This perspective is based on Revelation 7:9, which says that in Heaven there will be people from every tribe, kindred, nation, and tongue. Because of this passage, some believe that God intends the nations to remain distinct, even in eternity—although many believe (myself included) that ultimately our ethnicity doesn't define us, because in Christ and eternity there are no real distinctions (read Gal. 3:28).

One positive aspect of the salad bowl approach is that it protects both ethnic diversity and ethnic groups not fully accepted into the mainstream. For example, African American slavery, the Jim Crow laws, and racial prejudice stopped many blacks from being accepted into the mainstream, which forced them to develop a subculture within the American culture.

Amidst these positive traits, however, there are a few things to keep in mind. The United States is a social experiment born out of the Christian ethos of liberty and justice for all ethnic and religious groups. It is primarily made up of immigrants from other nations and has become a great nation because immigrants have adopted the cultural ethos and vision of the American dream. Thus, many ethnic groups have morphed into a melting pot, which has resulted in the greatest and the most influential nation in the world.

The United States is a social experiment born out of the Christian ethos of liberty and justice for all ethnic and religious groups.

Even though the United States has had major blemishes, it is still the greatest model of Revelation 7:9 the world has ever seen. Some black leaders I have spoken to who oppose the salad bowl approach argue that in spite of the horrible history of slavery and prejudice, past generations of blacks would not have been converted to Christianity if they had stayed in Africa, and they would not be enjoying the vast economic opportunities this nation affords. These same Black leaders also claim that the melting pot approach is the best model for the survival and strength of a nation, because a salad bowl approach would eventually result in the erosion of the nation's overarching Christian and American cultural ethos.

In contemporary society, we see the problems France has had with riots breaking out in over 200 cities because the Islamic population has not assimilated into the French or European culture. Some Muslim neighborhoods are even off-limits to the French police. I have friends who have been in cities near Paris who claim there are Muslim areas the French police are afraid to enter!

A Melting Pot

Melting Pot proponents say the salad bowl approach is really another form of racism and ethnic superiority, because they believe that in order to maintain ethnic identity, we must isolate our children from other ethnic groups and forbid interracial marriages. In Queens, New York, many of the Korean churches are losing their young people because they refuse to have services in English and adapt to Western culture. In the 1990s, Dr. Fred Price, a well-known television preacher and a graduate of Kenneth Hagin Sr.'s Rhema Bible School, took umbrage with Kenneth Hagin Jr. when Hagin said he was not in favor of "racially" mixed marriages. This incident caused a rift between them and damaged the brotherly relationship between Dr. Price, who is black, and the white Hagin family.

Many believe the salad bowl approach has gained strength because of the lack of transcendent Christian morals and purpose in our country during the past 50 years. Consequently, our political and educational institutions have adopted a relativistic approach where an individual's value is based solely on an ethnic identity and cultural nuance. Because culture involves belief systems and religion as well as common dress, food, language, and celebrations, multiculturalism can lead to polytheism, which in turn leads to moral relativism. This promotes anarchy, which then leads to totalitarianism, where people willingly give away their freedom in exchange for peace, safety, and security.

For example, Marxism advocates anarchy and an overthrowing of all religious values, which then leads to chaos and a revolution which paves the way for a totalitarian regime to take over. We saw this in the Bolshevik Revolution in 1917 in Russia, and in the various revolutions that preceded the advent of Communism in numerous countries in the 20th century, which became the bloodiest century in history because of this Marxist process!

Thus, we have seen over and over again that people will settle for tyrannical control over their life if there is a promise of peace, safety, and their economic needs being met.

Consequently, our political and educational institutions have adopted a relativistic approach where an individual's value is based solely on an ethnic identity and cultural nuance.

The Answer for the Human Heart

The truth is, we have all come from one blood; therefore, our differences are only skin deep. Harmony will only come when God's Kingdom principles have dominance in the human heart and rule over human relationships. We should respect and give honor to all human beings irrespective of ethnicity and cultural nuance. The Christian view is that *ethnicity* should be the word used to describe different people groups instead of the word *race*.

The truth is, we have all come from one blood; therefore, our differences are only skin deep.

God made many ethnic groups but only one human race. Consequently, all people should be given dignity as image-bearers of God. We shouldn't force assimilation and integration. At the same time, those of us who live in the United States should do all we can to uphold the biblical values that have made this nation great. In essence, we must give people from other nations and ethnicities the opportunity to live in our country and be granted the freedom to pursue the American dream of life, liberty, and the pursuit of happiness. The truth is, we are Christians first, and we are called to do all we can to perpetuate God's love and bless others with the freedom that God has given us to fulfill our God-given dreams, irrespective of gender and ethnicity.

We must note, however, that biblical justice does not include an egalitarian concept of forcing everyone to be equal and is not based on the false notion that "all men are created equal." The writers of the Declaration of Independence were referring to the fact that all people are image-bearers of God and should be treated with dignity and respect, but the reality is that all men are *not* created equal.

For example, if ten people ran a one-hundred meter dash, only one person would win. Someone else would come in last, thus proving that some are faster than others. We also know that not all people have the same IQ. Every person does not have the same physical and mental abilities. We are not equally called to be scientists, mathematicians, musical composers, singers, athletes, or artists, because God has given each of us gifting and ability in certain areas. Justice is not egalitarianism but a societal insistence that all people, irrespective of gender and ethnicity, have the equal opportunity to fulfill their God-given dreams.

Personally, I try to do all I can to promote ethnic unity within the Body of Christ, because according to John 17:21, unity is the greatest witness of the Gospel. No collection, class, or group of human beings will ever fully enjoy peace together outside of the local church; only the blood of Christ has the power to break down walls of division. (See Eph. 2:14; Gal. 3:28.) Furthermore, true unity is built upon trust. You can't fully love someone un-less you know him or her, and you can't know a person until you have a meaningful relationship with him or her. You can't have a deep relationship with a person unless trust develops over an extended period of time.

No collection, class, or group of human beings will ever fully enjoy peace together outside of the local church; only the blood of Christ has the power to break down walls of division.

Sometimes clashes between ethnic groups develop because authentic interaction between ethnic community leaders and their constituents is missing. Communication does not go be-yond the superficial political rhetoric they hear or read about in the media. Following the 48-hour "Building Bridges Retreat," our most significant conclusion was that in order for true racial reconciliation to take place, we needed to develop true relation-ships among ethnic leaders. For example, the Promise Keepers men's rallies of the 1990s were powerful prophetic gatherings that pointed the church back to the biblical unity that transcends ethnicity (see Gal. 3:28). They were not meant to be the end-all, but a catalyst for change. Many Christian leaders allowed a powerful Promise Keepers event at New York's Shea Stadium in 1995 to be the catalyst for long-lasting, Kingdom-building, multi-ethnic relations. I have intentionally built strong personal relationships with a number of the key African American lead-ers who are among my closest and dearest friends. As a result, we have partnered together to do significant things for the King-dom of God and the betterment of our dear city.

I agree with Dr. Martin Luther King Jr., who said that he longed for the day when people would not be judged by the color of their skin but by the content of their character:

> Five score years ago, a great American, in whose symbolic shadow we stand today, signed the Emancipation Proclamation. This momentous decree came as a great beacon light of hope to millions of Negro slaves who had been seared in the flames of withering injustice.... But one hundred years later, the Negro still is not free. One hundred years later, the life of the Negro is still sadly crippled by the manacles of segregation and the chains of discrimination....One hundred years later, the Negro is still languished in the corners of American society and finds himself an exile in his own land....But we refuse to believe that the bank of justice is bankrupt...I still have a dream. It is a dream deeply rooted in the American dream. I have a dream that one day this nation will rise up and live out the true meaning of its creed, "We hold these truths to be self-evident that all men are created equal." I have a dream that one day on the red hills of Georgia, the sons of former slaves and the sons of former slave owners will be able to sit down together at the table of brotherhood....I have a dream that my four little children will one day live in a nation where they will not be judged by the color of their skin but by the content of their character....I have a dream that...one day right there in Alabama little Black boys and Black girls will be able to join hands with little White boys and White girls as sisters and brothers. I have a dream today.[1]

As we conclude this chapter, we need to remember that all nations and languages will be represented in Heaven, and Heaven is a model for all Christians in their ethnically diverse relationships. We need to grapple with the secular idea of multiculturalism and why it is dangerous without an overarching Christian ethos. First and foremost, our identity must be rooted in Christ, and our relationships with one another should be based on God's definition of love—unconditional and all encompassing.

> *For as in one physical body we have many parts (organs, members) and all of these parts do not have the same function or use, so we, numerous as we are, are one body in Christ (the Messiah) and individually we are parts one of another [mutually dependent on one another]. Having gifts (faculties, talents, qualities) that differ according to the grace given us, let us use them* (Romans 12:4-6 AMP).

First and foremost, our identity must be rooted in Christ, and our relationships with one another should be based on God's definition of love—unconditional and all encompassing.

Think on This

As you consider the challenge of ethnic unity, begin to be more aware of the diversity around you.

1. What are the different ethnic groups represented in your:

   - Neighborhood?
   - Church family?
   - Work environment?

2. What can you do to become a bridge builder in each of these areas of influence?

3. Has your church or organization ever considered holding joint services, meetings, or social events with those of different ethnic backgrounds? If yes, what was the outcome? If no, what can you do to initiate such events?

4. What is the key element for overcoming racial divisions in your community, according to this chapter?

5. How are you going to begin to use this strategy to bring unity in your community?

Begin journaling your actions and the results you see.

Endnote

1. Dr. Martin Luther King Jr., transcription from "I Have a Dream Address," delivered August 28, 1963.

CHAPTER 3

PARTNERING FOR
CORPORATE DESTINY

Church and mission are not two distinct entities. They speak about the same reality. Whenever church and mission are presented as distinct entities, we tend to end up with dichotomies between ministry functions and competition among organizational structures.[1]

In January 2009, I celebrated my 25th year of serving Resurrection Church of New York as the senior pastor. Prior to January 1984, I functioned as an evangelist organizing large rallies and preaching on New York subway trains and on the Staten Island Ferry, which transports about 3,000 people to and from Staten Island and Brooklyn every day. After four years of intense personal evangelism and influencing thousands to make decisions for Christ, I came to the conclusion that to more effectively win and disciple people for Christ, I needed to build a strong local church. I found that new Christians needed a strong Christian family of families they could be connected to for faith sustainability and growth in applying biblical principles to their everyday lives.

> **I found that new Christians needed a strong Christian family of families they could be connected to for faith sustainability and growth in applying biblical principles to their everyday lives.**

Through the past quarter of a century, I have become even more convinced of the importance of a strong local church for both practical and theological reasons. Christian growth comes by individual Bible study and personal prayer but also through the grid of purposeful relationships with other Kingdom-minded individuals. Unfortunately, much of the preaching I hear on Christian television is about individual destiny, with messages such as, "How I can get my miracle," "How I can prosper," or "How I can write my own ticket with God." I have also found that the mission methodology of most para-church ministries is based on a sincere attempt to make disciples of Christ but without a proper emphasis on corporate destiny through active participation in a local church.

One case in point was when one of my dear friends asked me to attend a seminar that some national leaders (of a para-church ministry) were conducting in his church. Although the teaching and preaching contained great theological, cultural, sociological, and physiological insights on how to walk with God and fulfill personal destiny, it wasn't practical because none of it empha-sized the fact that an individual needs to submit to spiritual authority and function with other members of the Body of Christ in order to fulfill his or her destiny.

Individual destiny is not the primary focus in Scripture, since nearly all the promises in both the Old and New Testa-ments were either to Israel as a nation or to a local church in a particular city. Most promises God made were contingent upon the corporate body obeying and receiving a corporate blessing, or disobeying and causing a corporate curse. On most occasions when someone in Bible times heard Scripture read, it was usu-ally assumed that the words spoken were for God's covenant people as a whole, almost never to be extracted and applied to just one individual! If someone in the Old Testament was pun-ished for a sin by being put outside the camp, he or she was cursed because he or she could no longer partake of the corpo-rate covenant blessings (see Num. 12:14).

The New Testament continues this mind-set as we read that the Church is the rock that Christ has called to assail the gates of hell (see Matt. 16:18). *"And God placed all things under His feet and appointed Him to be head over everything for the church, which is His body"* (Eph. 1:22-23 NIV). It is *"the pillar and foundation of the truth"* and the center of God's purpose (1 Tim. 3:15 NIV). His Church will increase in in-fluence as God's Bride and the Holy City increase (see Rev. 21:2). The only practical way the local church can bring this about is by analyzing and then effectively ministering to the social, economic, and physical needs of their communities. The Church is the primary agent entrusted by God to steward the earth. We are to provide an image of God that nations, people, and groups can observe and desire to become a part of and partner with. What an awesome responsibility God has given to the Body of Christ!

The Church is the primary agent entrusted by God to steward the earth.

The apostle Paul encouraged the church in Corinth to stand together against the evil that existed in the city all around them by setting an example of unity and righteous living. *"Let a man regard us in this manner, as servants of Christ, and stewards of the mysteries of God"* (1 Cor. 4:1 NASB). Rather than just pointing to Heaven, the Church is to embody the Kingdom inside of them so that Christ's rule in the cosmos can be manifested on the earth (see Luke 17:21).

Partnering with Para-Church Ministries

In my study of Scripture, I have come to the conclusion that the Church has always been God's Plan A, never His Plan B. While some hyper-dispensationalists teach that the church was a parenthetical afterthought in the mind and heart of God, Scripture teaches us the purposes of God are administrated on the earth through the fullness of His body, which is the Church.

A dispensationalist believes that God deals with His people differently according to a certain dispensation of time, thus bringing discontinuity rather than continuity and unity to the Scriptures. My position is that the seed of God has always been connected by the various covenants, starting with the Cultural Commission in Genesis 1:28, irrespective of whether those involved were biological descendants of Abraham. (See Rom. 2:29; 9:6-8; 11:5-7.) The continuation of the covenants has come through the remnant, in which both Jew and Gentile have been reconciled in Christ and made into one new man, Christ's Body. (See Eph. 2:11-18; Gal. 3:28.)

It has always been my position that the Church has been the center of God's plan and purpose. Many who are frustrated at the lethargy of the church have moved on and either started para-church ministries or have bypassed the Church altogether to try and fulfill the Great Commission on their own. They attempt to reform society by going directly to university students, business-people, and the societal elite. As noble as that may sound, these people are in reality engaging in a mission without a biblical understanding of ecclesiology.

Although I believe para-church ministries were ordained by God and have been a blessing throughout Church history, I believe they need to take the attitude of John the Baptist when he said, *"He must increase, I must decrease"* (John 3:22-36). The main call of any para-church ministry should be to partner with local churches in order to aid and support that church's vision and call to disciple those in that church's sphere of influence and authority. Those who bypass the local church cause pastors to be suspicious, weaken the Body of Christ, and may actually act in competition with local churches. This counter-productive condition stifles the work of God in any region in which it occurs.

In my experience in 30 years of full-time church ministry, I have worked closely with both pastors and para-church leaders. Para-church leaders have had much frustration with pastors for not cooperating with their agendas; pastors have not trusted para-church ministries because often local church members who participate in para-church events become part of that ministry's future calls for volunteers, meetings, and finances. Some para-church ministries even advertise their events and their need for finances and volunteers directly to local church members without the knowledge or permission of the church leadership. Partnering involves mutual respect and open communication so that the work of the Kingdom is not stifled or hindered.

> **Partnering involves mutual respect and open communication so that the work of the Kingdom is not stifled or hindered.**

Kingdom Ecology

More and more Evangelical Christians are convinced that it is the responsibility of the Church to properly steward the ecosystems of the earth. Since the early 1990s, there has been a movement called "Creation Care" spearheaded by an Evangelical group called the Evangelical Covenant Church. The following is the overview of a resolution adopted by the annual meeting of the Evangelical Covenant Church in June 2007:

> There has never been a moment in human history in which we have not been intrinsically connected to and reliant upon all of God's creation. Recently, this interconnection has received heightened publicity, political debate, and biblical/theological study as we are becoming more and more aware of our effect on the global environment. There is urgency for improvement and change in how we practice creation-care for the air we breathe, the oceans we fish, the land we cultivate, and the water we drink so that we and the generations to come might live in sustainable and productive relationships with all of creation and fulfill our call to be good stewards. Therefore, the Young Pietists recommend that the 2007 Annual Meeting of the ECC resolves to encourage The Covenant to practice good stewardship of God's creation, and provide education and advocacy to this end.[2]

By ecology we mean the branch of biology dealing with the relations and interactions between organisms and other organisms, as well as with their environment.[3] While I don't personally believe there is conclusive proof that global warming is man-made, I do agree that there should be a "creation care" movement led by the Church because of our mandate from the Lord to *"steward the earth"* (see Gen. 1:27-28).

First of all, we need to appreciate the natural beauty of the environment around us because Psalm 19 teaches us that *"the heavens declare the glory of God; the skies proclaim the work of His hands"* (NIV). Since the skies are a witness of God's glory, we should work together to avoid veiling that glory with misty and murky, unhealthy pollution. All mankind should be able to look on the beauty of this world and see the awesomeness of God's handiwork.

Some years back I was blessed to be able to tour the island of Tahiti. It was so beautiful that I thought I was in the Garden of Eden! One of our guides kept referring to God as the creator of all that we saw around us. When I asked him why, he said, "In Tahiti there are no atheists because we know such incredible beauty could not have come without a master designer." He went on to tell us of his friend who was an atheist when he first came to live on the island, but within two weeks, became a believer in God after being exposed to the vast wonders of that island. I witnessed firsthand how the inhabitants of the island value and protect their environment so much that even the animals exhibited no fear toward humans. One day I was sitting by a river bed when a giant, 20-foot electric eel came up and put its gigantic head next to me so I could pet it.

Second, we should be concerned for the condition of the ecosystem of the earth because it's healthier for us as humans when the earth is clean. We have an obligation as Christians to lead the way with regard to maintaining the proper balance in the ecosystem by regulating the amount of chemical toxins that we put into our bodies, homes, and environment. The Book of Revelation teaches us that God *"destroys them that destroy the earth"* (Rev. 11:18 KJV). When we see news reports of marine life dying and washing onto our beaches or read statistics that indicate human cancer is on the rise in certain regions, we should immediately see the need for a collaborative effort to not only discover the cause of the imbalance but to also seek to rectify the situation. When there is so much smog in our cities that people are struggling to breathe, then it behooves the church to do something about it.

However, I must add a word of caution here, as overreacting to pollution and stopping the development of business is not the answer either. Hurting the economy also negatively affects the quality of life for everyone. We must work together with other organizations in our community for the good of all. Harmful pollutants and chemicals have become so integrated into the lifestyle of the modern world that reversing the production and effects of these harmful toxins is going to have to be a well thought out process employing the cooperative efforts of Christians, politicians, and business leaders. There is so much to be said about this point. I suggest you read both *Detoxify or Die* by Sherry Rogers and Don Colbert's book *What You Don't Know May Be Killing You.* See additional notes on some of the more common pollutants in the Appendix B portion of this book. Become aware and then become involved in effective Kingdom stewardship.

We must work together with other organizations in our community for the good of all.

Partnering for Kingdom Ecology

Finally, because the whole of the created order was reconciled back to God through the death of Christ on the cross, it
behooves us to have a solid scriptural foundation when it comes
to creation, ecology, and good stewardship. In this way, we can
interpret both our individual and corporate role in light of everything Christ reconciled to God through His death and resurrection! The following section of this chapter is designed to get
you started on building this firm foundation and to help you to
see the need for Christians to partner together to fulfill our corporate cultural commission.

> *And God blessed **them,** and God said unto **them,**
> Be fruitful, and multiply, and replenish the earth,
> and subdue it: and have dominion over the fish of the
> sea, and over the fowl of the air, and over every living
> thing that moveth upon the earth. And God said, Be-
> hold, I have given you every herb bearing seed, which
> is upon the face of all the earth, and every tree, in
> the which is the fruit of a tree yielding seed; to you
> it shall be for meat. And to every beast of the earth,
> and to every fowl of the air, and to every thing that
> creepeth upon the earth, wherein there is life, I have
> given every green herb for meat: and it was so. And
> God saw every thing that he had made, and, behold,
> it was very good* (Genesis 1:28-31 KJV).

Since this passage is the key verse expounded upon in this
book, I want to make sure it is pointed out that having dominion
over the earth is a call to steward every aspect of the planet,
including its ecosystems. After all, how would believers eat the
plants, fruits, seeds, and animals God gave us for food if they
were destroyed or contaminated by pollutants? Part of our call

to steward or have dominion is a call to protect our quality of food-producing elements by protecting the environment. Verse 31 says that God saw that everything He made was good. Biblical stewardship demands that we attempt to keep His creation in "good" condition! Notice, too, that this is a corporate call, as everything that God did and said was to and for *them.*

> *For it pleased the Father that in him should all fullness dwell; And, having made peace through the blood of his cross, by him to* **reconcile all things** *unto himself; by him, I say, whether they be things in earth, or things in Heaven* (Colossians 1:19-20 KJV).

We see here that Christ reconciled *all things* in Heaven and earth, not just individual souls. "Things" in this passage implies all material objects in time and space and immaterial objects that are spiritual in nature. By the way, when God says *all,* He means *all!*

> *For God so loved the* **world** *that He gave His only begotten Son, that whoever believes in Him should not perish but have everlasting life* (John 3:16).

Since the Greek word for *world* in this passage is "cosmos," the implications of this familiar verse are far reaching, since cosmos means the sum total of the material universe.[4]

> *[He planned] for the maturity of the times and the climax of the ages to* **unify all things** *and head them up and consummate them in Christ, [both] things in Heaven and things on the earth* (Ephesians 1:10 AMP).

This passage teaches that the ultimate goal of the Kingdom of God is the uniting together of *all things* both in Heaven and in earth in Christ—obviously, this includes the physical earth—not just the people who live in the earth. Because of this, we logically conclude that God so loved the material sum of the universe that He sent His Son to reconcile it *all* back to Him. Christians are concomitantly responsible to take the lead in loving the earth as well. We do not destroy the things we love; we take care of them.

Christians are concomitantly responsible to take the lead in loving the earth.

Leading the Way

God has given us biblical examples of those who have led the way and loved Creation as He does. As image-bearers of God, we need to understand His heart and then exemplify it in our daily walk. We must constantly be on the lookout for ways we can be an example of His love for all of creation. As you read through these brief biographies, begin to formulate how you can begin to function as a Kingdom leader in partnering for ecology.

Adam

> *And out of the ground the Lord God formed every beast of the field, and every fowl of the air; and brought them unto Adam to see what he would call them: and whatsoever Adam called every living creature, that was the name thereof. And Adam gave names to all cattle, and to the fowl of the air, and to every beast of the field* (Genesis 2:19-20 KJV).

Adam must have had an amazing mind, because there is no person alive today who would be able to catalogue names for the thousands of species on the earth! The fact that God put Adam through that meticulous process is also indicative of the fact that He puts great importance on the animals of creation. God's love for animals should also be extended to include caring for the environment, because without a balanced ecosystem, the animals will not be able to survive.

We can also surmise that, since Adam was the first person God commanded to have dominion over the plants, fruits, precious metals, and trees, it was the original intent for all of His people to continue to take the lead in caring for the environment and the whole created order. Genesis 2:12-15 teaches that God wanted Adam to till the Garden of Eden and keep it, and that this Garden included precious metals, as shown in verse 12.

> And the gold of that land is good: there is bdellium and the onyx stone. And the name of the second river is Gihon: the same is it that compasseth the whole land of Ethiopia. And the name of the third river is Hiddekel: that is it which goeth toward the east of Assyria. And the fourth river is Euphrates. And the Lord God took the man and put him into the garden of Eden to dress it and to keep it (Genesis 2:12-15 KJV).

Solomon

Solomon and Adam were both prophetic forerunners of Christ. Jesus was called the second or last Adam in First Corinthians 15:45, and Solomon was the wisest and most powerful man in the world. It is significant that both Adam and

Solomon showed a keen interest in stewarding God's creation. Scripture tells us that God gave Solomon exceedingly great wisdom and understanding and largeness of heart, even as the sand that is on the seashore (see 1 Kings 4:29). Solomon spoke 3,000 proverbs and sang over 1,000 songs, many of which were about the beauties of nature and God's creation (see 1 Kings 4:32).

People came from all over the world to hear of Solomon's wisdom as he taught about trees, animals, birds, insects, and marine life (see 1 Kings 4:33-34). The Book of Ecclesiastes even speaks about the vineyards, gardens, orchards, and numerous trees that he planted (see Eccles. 2:4-5). Truly the Scriptures teach that a wise and understanding person is a person who cares much about all of God's creation—not just about spiritual things. I believe caring for the created order is just as religious as many of the spiritual traditions and disciplines that Christians practice.

Truly the Scriptures teach that a wise and understanding person is a person who cares much about all of God's creation—not just about spiritual things.

In summary, we see that Adam was given the responsibility to care for all of creation. Solomon not only cared for creation but also taught with great wisdom so that those who would follow would understand God's definition of good stewardship. Two of the wisest men in the world were students and stewards of that created order. Of course, the greatest and wisest person who ever lived, Jesus Christ, actually died to reconcile the whole world, the cosmos or created order, back to the Father. Wise people should model their lives after these three men!

In light of our call to steward the created order, I think it is clear that Christians must partner together to fulfill the mandate from God to live out the Kingdom with regard to:

- The systems of the created order—politics, economics, sociology, education, media, family, law, art, religion, and all of the major components that make up the infrastructure of society.

- Creation care—the proper stewardship of the environment, including zoology, botany, marine life, anthropology, and geography.

- The health industry—including preventive health care through the use of proper nutritional habits, detoxifying your body, home, and environment, and the traditional medical profession.

- Space exploration—since Christ reconciled the heavens as well as the earth, the extraterrestrial universe is included in our field of stewardship.

- Things regarding all spiritual realities as related to believers and unbelievers.

Presently, this last item is the only field most Christians are focused on!

It should be very clear from the extent of the responsibility we have been given as God's representatives on the earth that we must work together to accomplish this mandate. How can we even think that we could begin to fulfill the cultural commission individually? The Father said it was not good for the first man to be alone and designed a helpmeet for him. Then He gave *them* the awesome job of overseeing not only a garden but the whole world. They were called to work together to fill the earth, subdue it, and have dominion over it.

> **It should be very clear from the extent of the responsibility we have been given as God's representatives on the earth that we must work together to accomplish this mandate.**

As we close this chapter, we need to understand that the local church has been appointed God's main entity to carry out His Kingdom purpose in our communities. As the fullness of God, the salt of the earth, and the light of the world, the Church is called to affect biblical transformation in the nations so that God's will is done on earth as it is in Heaven (see Eph. 1:23; Matt. 5:13-16). This will be done as individual believers connect to the corporate destiny of a local church in their communities and partner together to see His will be done on earth as it is in Heaven.

Think on This

Complete the following statements and then explain what they mean to you as a Christian leader called of God to affect biblical transformation in your community.

1. Church and mission are _Nut_ two distinct entities.

2. There is no such thing as _individc_ destiny in Scripture.

3. Every promise God made was contingent upon the _____*Corporate*_____ body obeying and receiving a _____*Corporate*_____ blessing.

4. Partnering involves mutual _____*RESPECT*_____ and _____*Mutual Open*_____ communication so that the work of the Kingdom is not stifled or hindered.

5. Harmful pollutants and chemicals have so integrated the lifestyle of the modern world that reversing these harmful toxins is going to have to be a well thought out process employing the _____*cooperative*_____ _____*Effort*_____ of Christians, politicians, and business leaders.

6. Finally, because the whole of created order was reconciled back to God through the death of Christ on the cross, it behooves us to have a solid scriptural foundation when it comes to _____*creation*_____, _____*equality*_____, and good _____*stewardship*_____.

Endnotes

1. Craig Van Gelder, *The Essence of the Church: A Community Created by the Spirit.* (Grand Rapids, Michigan: Baker Books, 2000), 31.

2. Presented by Adam Rohler, delegate from Bethesda Covenant Church, New York, New York, on behalf of the Young Pietists (The Evangelical Covenant Church, 2010), http://www.covchurch.org/resolutions/2007-creation-care.

3. "Ecology," *Dictionary.com Unabridged* (Random House, Inc., 2010), http://dictionary.reference.com/browse/ecology.

4. [kosmos /kos·mos/] AV translates as "world" 186 times, and "adorning" once. 1) An apt and harmonious arrangement or

constitution, order, government. 2) Ornament, decoration, adornment (i.e., the arrangement of the stars, "the heavenly hosts," as the ornament of the heavens [1 Pet. 3:3]). 3) The world, the universe. 4) The circle of the earth, the earth. 5) The inhabitants of the earth, men, the human race.

CHAPTER 4

PARTNERING WITHIN THE
APOSTOLIC REFORMATION

Anyone observing what is taking place in the religious world today can't help but notice the proliferation of what has been termed "the apostolic reformation." Because this is such an important move of God, we need to understand the term "apostolic" and how this relates to our discussion on partnering in the Kingdom of God.

> **Because this is such an important move of God, we need to understand the term "apostolic" and how this relates to our discussion on partnering in the Kingdom of God.**

Unfortunately, both historically and in contemporary times, we have seen abuse with regard to the presumptuous and even precocious use of this term, resulting in misunderstanding and alienation of many in the church when it comes to recognizing the apostolic model today. Furthermore, the term "apostolic," when describing a movement, also carries with it some unfortunate baggage because of the autocratic leadership style some have used while placing legalistic demands on their church members. My goal is to expound on the biblical definition of the term "apostolic" and God's purpose in giving this ministry gift to His Church.

> *It was he who gave some to be **apostles,** some to be prophets, some to be evangelists, and some to be pastors and teachers* (Ephesians 4:11 NIV).

I believe that all the ministry gifts mentioned in Ephesians 4:11 continue to exist and that there are many today who may have a legitimate claim to the ministry of apostle. An apostle in this context is someone who is a charismatic visionary and usually oversees a network of nondenominational congregations who have voluntarily placed themselves in submission to the apostle. (I also believe denominational leaders can be apostles, but I am dealing with movements—not denominations—in this section.) Two men I know well, Dr. John Kelly, the founder of the International Coalition of Apostles, and Dr. C. Peter Wagner, a noted author and former Fuller Seminary professor, have been catalysts in this movement. The premise is that God is restoring the fivefold ministry gift of apostle that is mentioned in Ephesians 4:11.

An apostle in this context is someone who is a charismatic visionary and usually oversees a network of nondenominational congregations who have voluntarily placed themselves in submission to the apostle.

In the past ten years, there has been a lot of talk about a new apostolic reformation. In this book, we are going to concentrate on understanding the function and flow of apostolic movements as a whole so we can relate it to our theme on partnering in the work and advancement of the Kingdom. Perhaps we can best describe this as a sort of *new wineskin* revolutionizing the church around the world.

Pros and Cons of the Apostolic Reformation Movement

This resurgence of apostleships is called both a movement and a reformation because of the proliferation of apostolic leaders and networks all over the world. We see this mainly in China, Latin America, and Africa, as well as in the United States. Many believe the Body of Christ is transitioning into a post-denominational period—something most prominent Evangelical and Pentecostal leaders deny, especially in the United States.

One Evangelical leader told me that those who believe this are limiting themselves by alienating denominational leaders. A Pentecostal leader told me that while many denominations are losing influence worldwide, Pentecostal denominations, such as the Assemblies of God and Church of God in Christ, are continuing to enjoy growth on a global scale. Estimates I have been given claim that Pentecostals are now the second largest Christian group in the world, at 600 million, with the largest being the Roman Catholic Church, claiming slightly over one billion adherents.

A common trait of members of the apostolic reformation is that they have new authority structures. For example, instead of the denominational bishop or superintendent for affiliated churches in a parish, apostolic leaders reach out to many churches (regardless of denominational affiliation) within their region. They nurture indigenous leaders by providing leadership training in local, church-based Bible institutions as opposed to sending leaders away to seminary for ministerial training. They are vision-driven, sacrificial, and highly motivated by the Great Commission found in Matthew 28:19. Their members participate in loud praise and worship with a musical band, usually leaving organ-based hymnody behind. Numerous gifts of the Holy Spirit manifest in their small groups and in some public worship gatherings, such as speaking in tongues and supernatural healings.

> **They nurture indigenous leaders by providing leadership training in local, church-based Bible institutions as opposed to sending leaders away to seminary for ministerial training.**

Many are entrepreneurial, with new financing and business ventures, transitioning from a nonprofit, offering-based mentality to a for-profit, revenue-based mentality. Church planting is another hallmark of this reformation. New churches are usually nondenominational and are led by a charismatic leader rather than relying on a denominational institution to embed a new leader. A denomination may even transfer their pastor to another parish every few years to discourage dependence on one particular person.

I heard noted Pentecostal historian Dr. Vinson Synon give a lecture at the Joint College of Bishops Congress in 2006 on the weaknesses of the apostolic reformation. In summary, he said that the notion that all denominations are dying and that the apostolic reformation is the only growing viable global Christian movement is overlooking the Pentecostal churches. All Pentecostal groups are growing dynamically all over the world. He also argued that in some cases their apostles are unaccountable. Synon was concerned that apostleships could become an elitist movement, with all the power in the hands of a few, yet many denominations also have a hierarchical philosophy of the episcopate and/or the priesthood. He also mentioned that he feels they don't recognize the power of the lay people.

I don't agree with him on some of these points, because I know apostolic leaders who have accountability, as well as pastors who have fled denominations because of inadequate relational accountability. I have also witnessed apostolic leaders recognizing the power of the Kingdom-minded marketplace apostolic movement, which is made up of lay people.

One of his biggest concerns with this movement seems to be territorial apostles. Synon claimed that the apostolic movement has been a disaster and churches in the apostleship movement that claim to be renewing have not grown. Again, I tend to disagree with such a generalization because church history shows that some denominational systems have been a disaster and many apostolic movements are presently experiencing tremendous growth.

Regarding some unethical practices, Synon points out some apostolic movements have tried to "buy off" and entice pastors and congregations to leave their denomination in return for financial support. I have heard of this happening in Cuba, but as a general rule, we should never judge a movement by its fringe.

A positive quality Vinson Synon mentioned about apostolic reformation is that it challenges denominations to be more mission-minded. They provoke true apostles to go into the world, and it gives new generations a fresh and exciting challenge. We need apostolic success more than we need apostolic succession. The secret to success is, of course, placing God's mission for the Church as the central theme in whatever we do, and working together to accomplish His purposes in our local communities and cities.

We need apostolic success more than we need apostolic succession.

In Ephesians 4:11-16, the apostle Paul clearly explains God's purpose for the five-fold ministry gifts.

> *And He gave some as apostles, and some as prophets, and some as evangelists, and some as pastors and teachers, **for the equipping of the saints for the work of service, to the building up of the body of Christ;** until we all attain to the unity of the faith, and of the knowledge of the Son of God, to a mature man, to the measure of the stature which belongs to the fullness of Christ. As a result, we are no longer to be children, tossed here and there by waves and carried about by every wind of doctrine, by the trickery of men, by craftiness in deceitful scheming; but **speaking the truth in love, we are to grow up in all aspects into Him who is the head,** even Christ, from whom the whole body, **being fitted and held together by what every joint supplies,** according to the proper working of each individual part, causes the growth of the body for the building up of itself in love* (Ephesians 4:11-16 NASB).

Defining an Apostolic Ministry

There are several factors involved in determining whether or not a ministry is apostolic in nature. I believe that the

---

apostolic movement is characterized by Bible-believing pastors and ministers voluntarily partnering together to advance the Kingdom of God, irrespective of their denominational affiliation or sectarian identities. These ministerial leaders emerge because they have an apostolic anointing that galvanizes the Body of Christ in their region and gives direction to city church movements.

> **I believe that the apostolic movement is characterized by Bible-believing pastors and ministers voluntarily partnering together to advance the Kingdom of God, irrespective of their denominational affiliation or sectarian identities.**

This might scare some denominational leaders who exercise leadership over certain ministers and churches because of political placement, organizational loyalty, seniority, or administrative ability. Their gifting might be more like that of an administrator than that of a pastor to pastors or an apostle; therefore, they might even see the apostolic movement as a threat. They may have witnessed ministers under their denominational authority gravitating toward those in their region who have the call of God on their lives to speak apostolically into the community or city and to assemble the Body of Christ to advance the Kingdom. Consequently, opposition against the apostolic is most likely fueled by certain religious leaders who believe it will undermine their influence in a region rather than because of theological disagreement.

> **Opposition against the apostolic is most likely fueled by certain religious leaders who believe it will undermine their influence in a region rather than because of theological disagreement.**

Another notable sign of apostolic reformation in these present times is when the regional church begins to demonstrate her unity publicly through various corporate events. These become visible expressions of the emerging "One City, One Church" reality in the Body of Christ. Such unity events as "Concerts of Prayer," "Community Development Projects," "Ministerial Associations," and "Pastors Covenant and Accountability Groups" bring pastors together for the good of the whole and start to change their mind-set and language regarding the church in general. They say things like, "One city, one church" or "One church, but many congregations," and they realize that a senior pastor is not primarily called to a local church but to shepherd or build a community for the Kingdom of God.

This united church then begins to speak prophetically to the culture, influencing all of society, not just the church world. Crime drops, and elected officials start coming to apostolic and prophetic leadership for prayer, counsel, and political support. The spiritual climate of a community begins to change as the Word of God once again becomes the standard and rule of law for the community.

An apostolic church would have a strong apostolic leader functioning as the senior pastor. These churches employ a form of church government that involves a plurality of leaders under the leadership of an apostolic leader. Although this leadership or ministry team may have different names, such as eldership team, ministry team, or deacon board, they all flow out of the paradigm of a "multiplicity of ministries" instead of the "mom and pop shop" mode of church government that has been so commonly employed by many congregations. An apostolic church would continually send out ministers to plant churches and start new ministries that holistically affect whole communities and place godly leadership in every sphere of society for the purpose of fulfilling the Great Commission.

An apostolic church would continually send out ministers to plant churches and start new ministries that holistically affect whole communities and place godly leadership in every sphere of society for the purpose of fulfilling the Great Commission.

Apostolic churches nurture and mother other pastors, ministers, and churches. Their primary concern is partnering with other Christians to build the Kingdom of God and not their own entities. They have learned to work and bless the Body of Christ in their locale; and they know they are called of God to serve the Kingdom, not just their local flock. Consequently, the whole community rises to another level, and the Body of Christ as a whole experiences growth.

This is in stark contrast to some mega-churches that sometimes grow from gaining new members from the smaller "feeder churches" in their area because they have more programs to offer. Instead of seeing how they can share their resources, minister to the pastors of smaller churches, and help equip them to be more effective in their region, some of these churches actually focus the marketing of their ministry to the attendees of these smaller churches. They don't target the lost, but concentrate on building their mailing list at the expense of many of the congregations around them. Though their church may experience tremendous growth, the Kingdom is not enlarged, and they are merely "swapping fish" and building empires rather than promoting God's Kingdom.

This is not meant to be a polemic that engenders a judgmental attitude toward certain churches or denominations, but it is meant to provide a greater understanding of perhaps the most important reformation we have seen since the first tangible evidence of the Protestant Reformation in 1517. Let's not forget that there are also variations within each group and movement. We are forced to merely classify and categorize but not reflect on every possible situation within a movement or church.

For example, some apostolic movements are very loose, with little organization and financial commitments. Others are well organized, require tithes or fees, credential their members, provide covering, and may even gather around some body of theological agreement. I have presented a comparison of the strengths and weaknesses of historic denominationalism versus the current apostolic movement in the appendix that accompanies this chapter.[1]

Denominational and Apostolic Partnering

Although I do not presently belong to a denomination, I have a great deal of respect for all of them, especially as I study their early history. There is a lot of truth and wisdom to glean for those of us in the apostolic reformation and independent Evangelical church. Among other things, they have a connection to

historic creeds, confessions, and church history, they have infil-
trated and gained credibility in cultural institutional systems,
and they have a system of ordination, placement of ministry, and
criteria for ministry training. They started as a movement and
have cycled into an institution; thus they are ahead of the usual
cyclical norm. They have an understanding of culture and academia along with theology and don't have an anti-intellectual
bias in their churches. Many denominations are also involved in
lobbying public policy issues.

I believe those of us in the apostolic reformation would be
wise to learn from mainline Christian denominational history,
namely their successes and failures, so we can mimic their
strengths and avoid their weaknesses. Apostolic leaders and
churches need to rejuvenate a love for historic church writings,
including the creeds, confessions, and theological writings of the
church fathers during the church's first six centuries.

> **I believe those of us in the apostolic
> reformation would be wise to learn from
> mainline Christian denominational
> history, namely their successes
> and failures, so we can mimic their
> strengths and avoid their weaknesses.**

We need to believe, according to Ephesians 4:11-16, that God
has been building and the Holy Spirit has been teaching His
Church for the past 2,000 years. Claiming ignorance of these
writings is to dismiss God's historic activity in His Church, and
it hinders our ability to build upon the shoulders of those who
have gone before us. I believe we need to have both a movement
and an institution, so that our movement can institutionalize

the ground we gain in the culture. Remaining merely a movement will marginalize us by keeping us on the fringe of society instead of infiltrating and reforming it.

In addition, I believe key apostolic leaders need to convene an assembly so that we can propose how to ordain and recognize clergy as apostolic leaders and bishops. Too often, many of us are self-appointed because there has not been a universally established protocol. One leader can only make a proposal, but if key leaders make a unified statement (like the Lausanne Covenant), other leaders will be pressured to follow their recommendations. Recognized apostolic leaders in a region should endorse and be a part of the process of setting a leader as a bishop or an apostle. I was consecrated as a bishop and apostolic leader in 2006 by many national and local leaders in the New York region.

Recognized apostolic leaders in a region should endorse and be a part of the process of setting a leader as a bishop or an apostle.

Since all denominations once started off as an apostolic movement driven by a powerful, visionary leader, we should learn how to allow for the cycle of "movement to maintenance to institutionalization" without compromising the missiological nature that gave it birth. This can be done by a continual emphasis on revival and renewal; keeping a steady flow of prayer, fasting, and worship; allowing God to burden and activate us for missions and reformation; and continuing to nurture our spiritual and biological children. We can remain on the cutting edge of what God is doing on the earth in this generation as we partner with each other and learn from those who have gone before us.

There are many ways we can partner together, denominational and apostolic, for the equipping of the Body of Christ. For example, both denominational and apostolic congregations often lose their children to the world because the media present a comprehensive humanistic worldview, while our values are often issue-driven and fragmented. When our children see the Body of Christ in competition with one another, we aren't teaching the next generation according to Deuteronomy 6:6-8. Both in word and in lifestyle we need to first and foremost exemplify the Kingdom of God on the earth. When we declare we are the eye and that the ear is not important, we bring division to the Body of Christ and merely prove that our lives are inconsistent with what we preach. This produces a rebellious nature in our offspring and leaves them open to the influences of non-Christian mind-sets.

When we declare we are the eye and that the ear is not important, we bring division to the Body of Christ and merely prove that our lives are inconsistent with what we preach.

Though admittedly there are distinct differences in our approach to fulfilling the cultural commission, both denominational and apostolic leaders do have some things in common. Both groups should return to studying systematic and biblical theology and apologetics. Up and coming leaders should be trained with a biblical worldview that is capable of advancing them through the highest universities in academia. Instead of being anti-intellectual and running from academia, we should be infiltrating and helping lost academicians to return to their original purpose.

Many apostolic leaders are biblicists who are not well read or well-rounded. They are often unable to prepare, equip, and relate to those who lead various realms of our society. Many denominational congregations do not have the anointing of the apostolic to affect large regional areas. Think of the cultural impact of the two working together and realizing we are one body with many members—one church but many congregations!

The next advance for both the apostolic and denominational leaders will be to go from understanding the missiological nature of the Church and our call to have dominion, to applying the biblical worldview to public policy. This will mean that leaders will have to hold the newspaper in one hand and the Bible in the other. We will have to do the grunt work of engaging our culture, not just having worldview conversations with other Christians.

We need to go from speaking dominion to exercising influence in the marketplace of ideas. After all, since the Bible speaks truth to every realm of society, we should expect to win and lead in a democratic meritocracy. By respecting the call of God on our respective ministries, we can partner together and not only protect our own but also advance the Kingdom of God on the earth.

We need to go from speaking dominion to exercising influence in the marketplace of ideas.

As we conclude this chapter, we should contemplate and come to understand what the present apostolic reformation is, and the difference between a denomination and an apostolic network. We also need to be aware of the weaknesses and strengths of both apostolic and denominational networks. More importantly, we need to ask ourselves if a new synthesis can take place between the two to maximize our potential and more effectively fulfill the cultural commission for our communities and cities.

Think on This

1. Do you know anyone today who functions apostolically?

2. Is your local church a denominational or apostolic church? (See Appendix A for a quick comparison of the two.)

3. Do you now believe it is important to pursue a partnership with either a denominational or an apostolic church? Why or why not?

4. How is what you learned in this chapter going to affect your leadership position in the Body of Christ?

Endnote

1. See Appendix A for a summary of generalizations from an article I wrote entitled "Apostolic Movements and Institutions." This position paper may be found under the teachings on my Web site, www.josephmattera.org.

CHAPTER 5

PARTNERING FOR THE PROGRESS
OF THE KINGDOM

*Making known to us the mystery (secret) of His will
(of His plan, of His purpose). [And it is this:] In accordance with His good pleasure (His merciful in-
tention) which He had previously purposed and set
forth in Him, [He planned] for the maturity of the
times and the climax of the ages to unify all things
and head them up and consummate them in Christ,
[both] things in heaven and things on the earth*
(Ephesians 1:9-10 AMP).

Throughout church history there has always been a major
difference of opinion regarding the last days and the consummation of the age. I am sure these potential divisions will

remain until the day Christ returns. But we can not allow these differing world viewpoints to keep us from being unified within the Body of Christ. As we study these different end-time philosophies, it is important to understand that Jesus taught the gradual victory of His Kingdom on earth. He taught us, *"When ye pray, say, 'Our Father which art in Heaven, Hallowed be thy name. Thy Kingdom come. Thy will be done, as in Heaven, so in earth'"* (Luke 11:2 KJV). He also taught His disciples that the church would prevail against the *"gates of hell"* (Matt. 16:18 KJV). History teaches us that the church has always risen to the top with regard to cultural influence, even though there may have been long periods of time when her influence in particular nations looked bleak. We must be cautious as we anticipate the consummation of the age that we do not neglect the cultural mandate God gave us in Genesis 1:28.

In my more than 30 years of being a Christian, I have heard many stories of folks who opted out of engaging the culture because they believed that they were living in the endtimes and that they should only focus on getting people saved. The problem with this mind-set, of course, is that these new Christians also need to grow. If the church only focuses on evangelism, many will come to know Jesus as Lord and Savior but will never learn to walk in power and dominion. They will basically live the same lives they have been living and watch the sky for the return of Jesus. There will be no substantial change in their families, communities, or cities.

If the church only focuses on evangelism, many will come to know Jesus as Lord and Savior but will never learn to walk in power and dominion.

One family that was very instrumental in winning many young people to Christ in my community moved away from New York City to a remote farmland because they were afraid the end was here and that New York City was going to get destroyed by a nuclear attack when Russia invaded Israel in fulfillment of Ezekiel 38-39. Many Christians interpret Gog and Magog to be modern Russia—something that has no exegetical or historical support but was a popular teaching of a book by Hal Lindsey called *The Late Great Planet Earth* that influenced millions of Evangelical Christians in the 1970s.

Another person I know left college and missed out on getting a higher education to go out and evangelize because, "Jesus is coming any day now!" A very successful businessman I know sold his businesses, gave the money away, and began witnessing to everyone he met. This eventually grew into a congregation, which he felt God was calling him to oversee. What he did was influenced by a false view regarding his belief that the end of the world was near, and he now regrets the fact that he walked away from a huge income stream that could have been a great blessing to the church he is presently overseeing.

Beware of the Modern Escapist Theology

One of the greatest theological issues many of us have had to grapple with is how we view the endtimes. Views within Christian orthodoxy vary from hyper-dispensational, dispensational, pre-millennialism, and post-millennialism to a classical millennium position. Each view poses different theories with regard to such questions as: will the church decrease, will it apostatize and be rescued via the rapture before the second coming of Christ, or will the church continue to experience gains, progress, and eventually have a rampant international Kingdom witness that will restore all things? (See Acts 3:20-21.)

Truly one's eschatology, or understanding of the endtimes, will determine one's teleology, or goals in this life. I do want to make a point to say that all views within orthodox Christianity are insightful, and each view seeks support from Scripture. However, I also want to warn Christians not to resort to a modern escapist theology. We should never think that the Evangelical church will become irrelevant with regard to societal reform. There could be grave dangers for our world if we determined only to escape this "hellish" world to arrive at a better "heavenly" place. We were each born for a reason, and to disregard our purpose for this world is to disregard God's thoughts during our creation![1]

Truly one's eschatology, or understanding of the endtimes, will determine one's teleology, or goals in this life.

We are assured and know that [God being a partner in their labor] all things work together and are [fitting into a plan] for good to and for those who love God and are called according to [His] design and purpose. For those whom He foreknew [of whom He was aware and loved beforehand], He also destined from the beginning [foreordaining them] to be molded into the image of His Son [and share inwardly His likeness], that He might become the firstborn among many brethren. And those whom He thus foreordained, He also called; and those whom

*He called, He also justified (acquitted, made righ-
teous, putting them into right standing with Himself). And those whom He justified, He also glorified
[raising them to a heavenly dignity and condition or
state of being]* (Romans 8:28-30 AMP).

Because the purpose of this chapter is not to get into specific
eschatological positions such as pre-, post-, or a-millennialism,
I simply want to share why my attitude toward the progress of
the Kingdom of God on this side of Heaven is purposeful and op-
timistic and how we can partner together to fulfill His ultimate
purpose for our lives and His Church.

The Church and Israel

Where we land on determining who we think is ultimately
called to fulfill the cultural mandate and manifest the Kingdom
of God on earth will also determine the amount of influence we
will have on earth. Failure to resolve this issue as to whether the
future "saved" nation of Israel or the present worldwide Church
is responsible could be detrimental to attaining our individual
and corporate destinies.

If we believe that the people who will one day be restored in
Israel are responsible for the earth, then we have a philosophical
excuse for staying in survival mode, merely waiting to be rescued
by Jesus in the rapture. This, of course, also implies that He is
returning for a defeated, fragmented church instead of a united
Church without spot or wrinkle as described in Ephesians 5:27.
The Kingdom of God was meant to be manifested in this dispensation by the "seed of God," which was formerly comprised solely
of Jews, yet which is presently comprised of the Body of Christ
made up of "called out" Jewish and Gentile believers in Jesus the
Messiah.

*No man who believes in Him [who adheres to, relies on, and trusts in Him] will [ever] be put to shame or be disappointed. [No one] **for here is no distinction between Jew and Greek.** The same Lord is Lord over all [of us] and He generously bestows His riches upon all who call upon Him [in faith]. For **everyone** who calls upon the name of the Lord [invoking Him as Lord] will be saved* (Romans 10:11-13 AMP).

The *hyper-dispensational pre-millennial view* espoused by Darby, *Scofield Bible, Ryrie Study Bible,* D.L. Moody, Henry Thiessen, Louis Sperry Chafer, and (in the recent past) Dallas Theological Seminary teaches that Israel and the church have two separate callings and two separate destinies. Along with an attempt to literally interpret certain passages in the Old Testament, the primary passage used to articulate this view is found in Daniel 9:24-27.

They focus on verse 26, which says that the Jewish time clock stops at 69 weeks, which opens the way for the advent of the Church as a "parenthetical" body of people who will be raptured once the Jewish clock begins ticking again, which includes the advent of the tribulation and revelation of the antichrist in the beginning of the seventieth week as described in verse 27. Thus, a remnant of the Jews who are left after the Church is caught up to Heaven will be converted and begin to evangelize the rest of the nations until Christ comes to save all of Israel at the end of the 70th week.

And after the sixty-two weeks [of years] shall the Anointed One be cut off or killed and shall have nothing [and no one] belonging to [and defending] Him. And the people of the [other] prince who will come will destroy the city and the sanctuary. Its end shall come with a flood; and even to the end there shall be war, and desolations are decreed. And he shall enter into a strong and firm covenant with the many for one week [seven years]. And in the midst of the week he shall cause the sacrifice and offering to cease [for the remaining three and one-half years]; and upon the wing or pinnacle of abominations [shall come] one who makes desolate, until the full determined end is poured out on the desolator (Daniel 9:26-27 AMP).

This passage will make more sense if the reader understands that each day symbolically equals one year and each week equals seven years. Thus, it is teaching that 483 years after the rebuilding of the temple under Ezra, the Messiah appears and God's dealings with Israel stop because they reject Him. This makes room for the Church age to start, until the time clock for the Jews starts again for the final week or seven years, which starts with the great tribulation after the Antichrist is revealed. This viewpoint makes the Church nothing more than a parenthetical blip until the purposes of God on the earth are restarted through Israel.

Up until hyper-dispensational views came on the scholarly scene in the 19th century, most scholars believed that the entire 70 weeks of Daniel had already been fulfilled. (Only dispensationalists believe the entire 70th week is a future event.) In my view, the time clock started in 458 B.C. with the decree by Persian King Artaxerxes to send Ezra the Jewish priest to rebuild Jerusalem (see Ezra 7:13-26).

Sixty-nine weeks or 483 years from the time of this event would be A.D. 26, the time many accept as the date when the Holy Spirit fell on Jesus as He commenced His earthly ministry. After the events of the last or 70th week, seven years commence, which include Christ making a covenant with His people by dying on the cross (the midst of the week in the spring of

A.D. 30). (See Daniel 9:27.) The 490 years would end three years later, after the birth of the church and the stoning of Stephen, which sealed the fate of the Jewish nation's judgment for rejecting Christ. Daniel 9:26-27 shows that their desolation was determined or decreed during this time. It came to pass in A.D. 70 when the Roman armies came and sacked Jerusalem and destroyed the temple and the genealogical records, ending the Old Testament levitical system.

God's Seed

Those like me with a *Reformed perspective* believe that starting from Adam, there has always been an antithesis between God's seed and satan's seed. In Genesis 3:15, after Adam and Eve disobeyed and ate of the Tree of the Knowledge of Good and Evil, God said to the serpent, *"I will put enmity between you and the woman, and between your seed and hers; he will crush your head and you will strike his heel"* (Gen. 3:15 NIV).

God's "seed" are the children of Abraham who became God's covenant witness connecting both testaments on the earth. Galatians 3:29 says, *"If you belong to Christ, then you are Abraham's seed, and heirs according to the promise"* (NIV). Thus, the real issue is not who is biologically descended from Abraham, but who is part of the seed of God from the time of God's promise of redemption to Adam. *"For God so loved the world, that he gave his only begotten Son, that **whosoever** believeth in him should not perish, but have everlasting life"* (John 3:16 KJV). The following verses show that it wasn't the biological ethnicity that caused a person to be a Jew but the same thing that justifies the present Church—faith and a circumcised heart.

In Acts 7:38, Stephen calls Israel, *"the church in the wilderness,"* implying that the words *Israel* and *church* are interchangeable, but also includes God's new "Gentile" church. The fact that Israel is called *"the church in the wilderness"* dispels the false notion that God had a separate plan for the church and Israel; they were both identified as God's seed or remnant because they were connected to God by faith in Jehovah.

The fact that Israel is called *"the church in the wilderness"* dispels the false notion that God had a separate plan for the church and Israel; they were both identified as God's seed or remnant because they were connected to God by faith in Jehovah.

Hebrews 4:2 says that Israel had the Gospel preached to them. Galatians 3:8 says God *"preached the Gospel beforehand to Abraham,"* thus showing the Gospel and Church in both testaments. This illustrates even further the fact that the Old Testament law contained the Gospel in shadow form in which a person needed to believe in the coming Messiah by faith as illustrated in the ceremonial law, such as having faith in the blood of the sacrificial lamb during the first Passover.

Furthermore, Paul said in Romans:

> *Not as though the word of God hath taken none effect. For they are not all Israel, which are of Israel: Neither, because they are the seed of Abraham, are they all children: but, In Isaac shall thy seed be called. That is, they which are the children of the flesh, these are not the children of God: but the children of the promise are counted for the seed* (Romans 9:6-8 KJV).

And in Romans 2:28-29 Paul explains:

For he is not a Jew, which is one outwardly; neither is that circumcision, which is outward in the flesh: But he is a Jew, which is one inwardly; and circumcision is that of the heart, in the spirit, and not in the letter; whose praise is not of men, but of God (Romans 2:28-29 KJV).

This again illustrates the fact that a person was not considered a Jew to God just because they were physical descendants of Abraham; they also had to believe the Gospel by having faith in the coming Messiah.

The Progress of the Kingdom of God

I believe that there are six specific reasons why the Kingdom of God will progress in time and space in human history:

1. We have learned that Genesis 1:28 was for the influence of God's Kingdom over the whole created order. This covenant contained the original purpose God had for Adam and his seed, and initiated the cultural commission.

2. We've noted that the dominion theme was never nullified in future covenants after the Fall, but rather, it was reconfirmed to the patriarchs and then to the Church, thus continuing the cultural commission theme into the New Testament.[2]

3. Revelation 21:1-4 shows the Kingdom of God progressing in history, totally changing the earth until the last enemy (death) is destroyed, which will usher in the eternal state. The Greek word for new in "new Heaven" is

kainos, which means qualitatively new as contrasted with *neos*, which means numerically new. That is to say, this verse in not speaking about a totally new and different earth but an old earth renewed by the progressive influence of Heaven joining with the earth through the influence of the Church! It is the fulfillment of Luke 11:2: *"Thy Kingdom come, thy will be done on earth as it is in Heaven."* This interpretation is in harmony with the passages in Revelation 21:1 and Isaiah 65:17-25, which clearly show that the new Heaven and new earth cannot be speaking solely about the eternal state, but about a period of time on the earth when God's presence and principles rule. In eternity there is no more death; however, in Isaiah 65:20, there is longevity of the human lifespan but still physical death. This proves the fact that this passage cannot only refer to the eternal state when time is no more! Even if someone lives well past 100, the fact that they die shows that they are still not living in eternity; hence, Revelation 21:1-4 is probably referring to the process of restoration coming to the earth through the progressive influence of the Gospel through the Church until "there is no more death, crying or pain for the former things are passed away"—which is the culmination of the victory of the Gospel in eternity (thus it refers to both a renewed earth and the eventual eternal state).

Revelation 21:1-4 shows the Kingdom of God progressing in history, totally changing the earth until the last enemy (death) is destroyed, which will usher in the eternal state.

4. Biblical hermeneutics teach us that we must interpret Scripture in light of Scripture. Although we may have differences of opinion with regard to the details of some of our eschatological positions, one thing all the covenants demonstrate is that thematically Scripture teaches that the Kingdom will continue to increase.

For unto us a Child is born, Unto us a Son is given; And the government will be upon His shoulder. And His name will be called Wonderful, Counselor, Mighty God, Everlasting Father, Prince of Peace. **Of the increase of His government and peace There will be no end,** *Upon the throne of David and over His Kingdom, To order it and establish it with judgment and justice From that time forward, even forever. The zeal of the Lord of hosts will perform this* (Isaiah 9:6-7 KJV).

I believe that by interpreting Scripture in light of Scripture, we see an irrefutable over-arching theme regarding the progressive victory of the Kingdom of God. We may not agree with how each verse is interpreted, but by concentrating on the macro themes from Genesis through Revelation, there can be unity in the Body of Christ, which leads me to my fifth point.

5. Scripture perpetuates the theme of progressive Kingdom victory. Psalm 110:1 teaches that the Messiah will sit at the right hand of the Father until His enemies are made His footstool. I constantly tell people that the time of the end is not soon, because the Church has a long way to go before it puts down the enemies of God as His Kingdom agents. Before somebody can tell me that the end is near, they are going to have to prove to me that all of Jesus' enemies have been made His footstool. They are going to have to illustrate how the nations of the world

are presently under the influence of the Kingdom of God and not primarily under the world system of satan. Psalm 110:2 says that He will rule out of Zion over His enemies. (Since Galatians 6:16 calls the Church *"the Israel of God,"* and Hebrews 12:22 refers to the Church as the heavenly Jerusalem and Mount Zion, it seems as though we are the "Zion" to which this psalm refers.) In Matthew 16:18, Jesus taught that the *"gates of hell"* will not prevail against the Church. Matthew 24:14 teaches that the time of the end will come after the Gospel of the Kingdom is preached in all the nations. There will be some kind of strong manifestation of God's Kingdom in each of the nations, which is much more than just the distribution of Bibles and Gospel tracts and having Gospel crusades and a television ministry. A Kingdom implies government; thus the Kingdom witness should include godly systems influencing and transforming secular societies.

In the parables of Jesus recorded in Matthew Chapter 13, Jesus taught that the Kingdom will continue to progress in the earth until all those near will benefit from it. In Matthew 13:31, Jesus compares the Kingdom of God to a mustard seed that starts out small but eventually becomes a tree large enough for the birds of the air to rest on. In Matthew 13:33, Jesus compares the Kingdom of God to the small amount of yeast that a woman puts in her bread dough, yet it proliferates throughout the whole lump. The Kingdom of God will bear fruit, multiply, and increase until the whole earth is influenced by it.

The Kingdom of God will bear fruit, multiply, and increase until the whole earth is influenced by it.

Some say that the yeast in Matthew 13:33 is a symbol of sin and that this parable is merely teaching that sin is going to continue to increase in the earth and be victorious. However, this interpretation is not congruent with the text because the subject of the parable is the Kingdom of God and not sin. It does not fit the flow of the previous parable of the sower in Matthew 13:1-9, in which the Word of God increased up to one hundredfold and was victorious.

6. I think it's important to note that church history clearly demonstrates that, against all odds, the church has always been victorious. From its inception, with the whole of the Roman Empire against it, the church not only survived but also became the dominant religion in only three centuries. After the fall of Rome with the barbarian conquest of A.D. 476, though many of the other facets of civilization were wiped out, the church again gained the ascendancy to convert the barbarians and lay the groundwork for the modern nations by A.D. 1000.

During the time of the Enlightenment in the 13th to 15th centuries, paganism looked as though it would conquer the church. But then God raised up Martin Luther, who started the Protestant Reformation that eventually swept across the whole known world. In our own nation after the Revolutionary War, the church declined so much that there were some who predicted Christianity would no longer exist by the mid-1800s. But God sent the Second Great Awakening through Charles Finney and others, which resulted in the transformation of our nation and the impetus for revivals that are still impacting the nations and the church to this day.

While the present church is now in decline in influence throughout much of Western Europe, it is burgeoning and gaining unprecedented growth in China, South Korea, parts of Indonesia, Southern Africa, Central and Latin America, and other parts of the world. Throughout history, the church has always had its ups and downs but eventually gains ascendancy and emerges as victorious. The schemes of the enemy are designed to divide and then conquer the Body of Christ. Though there are major differences of opinion regarding the last days and the consummation of the age, we cannot let them keep us from being unified in the Body of Christ. Jesus said a house divided against itself cannot withstand the attacks of the enemy (see Matt. 12:25).

Though there be major differences of opinion regarding the last days and the consummation of the age, we cannot let them keep us from being unified in the Body of Christ.

Obviously, Jesus expected His church to continue the work He began while He was here on the earth. He not only told His disciples to go into all the world and preach the good news to all creation, He also promised to equip them to accomplish it. John 14:12-14 indicates Jesus expected His church to become stronger and progressively more influential in the world.

*I assure you, most solemnly I tell you, if anyone steadfastly believes in Me, he will himself be able to do the things that I do; and **he will do even greater things than these,** because I go to the Father. And I will do [I Myself will grant] whatever you ask in*

My Name [as presenting all that I AM], so that the Father may be glorified and extolled in (through) the Son. [Yes] I will grant [I Myself will do for you] whatever you shall ask in My Name [as presenting all that I AM] (John 14:12-14 AMP).

Finally, many hyper-dispensationalists teach that the world will not be evangelized until the Jewish nation gets converted. Their belief is that the 144,000 who come to Christ in Revelation 7:1-9 points to the conversion of Israel and subsequent evangelization of the nations. But many believe this has already been fulfilled beginning in Acts 2 because it is symbolic of the remnant seed of God coming to Christ during and after the Day of Pentecost and then evangelizing the nations.

I believe Romans 11:25-26 teaches that instead of the nations waiting for Israel to evangelize them, Israel will be provoked to jealousy and convert to Christ after they see numerous nations coming to Christ. Though many English translations use the word Gentiles in Romans 11:25b-25, the *Concordant Literal Translation of the Bible* renders these verses: "until the complement of the *nations* may be entering. And thus all Israel shall be saved..."[3]

Think on This

As we conclude this chapter, we need to understand that the ultimate victory of the Church is the major theme of the biblical covenants, and that Jesus taught the gradual victory of His Kingdom on earth.

1. Look up each of the following Scriptures and then describe in your own words what God is teaching you in relation to

the progress of the Kingdom here on the earth and your part in accomplishing His purposes.

- Luke 11:2
- Ephesians 1:10
- First Corinthians 15:23-28
- Galatians 3:29

2. How has your hope for the future been affected by this chapter?

Endnotes

1. If you seek further study on this, my book *Ruling in the Gates* and Donald Dayton's book *Discovering an Evangelical Heritage* delve into the issue more extensively.

2. See chapters 3 and 4 in my book *Kingdom Revolution* for further study on this.

3. *The Concordant Literal New Testament,* http://www. concordant.org/version/NewFiles/06_Romans.htm.

CHAPTER 6

PARTNERING UNDER THE
LAW OF THE KINGDOM

In order to live out the cultural mandate to disciple whole nations, we must have biblical principles applicable to every
sphere of life as our blueprint. We must know what the Bible
teaches and then become strong leaders in areas such as economics, history, math, science, politics, family, self-government,
art, the military, education, children, and healthcare. Instead of
looking at the Bible as a roadmap to escape the earth, as dis-
cussed in the previous chapter, we need to study to show ourselves approved, finding ways to join together to lead others to
inherit the promises and blessings of the Kingdom.

We also must learn how to operate within the Law of the
Kingdom and yet operate with the civil law of our respective areas of influence. One of the great sections in the Bible for understanding Kingdom law is Exodus 20-23. Chapter 20 lays out the

Ten Commandments, and chapters 21-23 extrapolate the commandments and apply them specifically to civil law.

The Ten Commandments

In examining Exodus 20 carefully, we can see that the Ten Commandments are not just a moral code for individuals. These verses clearly show that these commandments are to serve as a blueprint for the whole nation of Israel regarding their vertical relationship with God and their horizontal relationship with their fellow man. Not only do the Ten Commandments provide spiritual health, but they are also connected to a nation's economics, personal freedom, and prosperity. If a nation keeps these laws, they will experience unprecedented economic prosperity and achieve a high view of personal freedom, which will allow them to use their God-given gifts and talents along with their entrepreneurial abilities and creativity to worship Him and advance His Kingdom.

> **If a nation keeps these laws, they will experience unprecedented economic prosperity and achieve a high view of personal freedom, which will allow them to use their God-given gifts and talents along with their entrepreneurial abilities and creativity to worship Him and advance His Kingdom.**

As a matter of fact, the first two verses of Exodus 20 show that God delivered Israel out of Egypt primarily for economic reasons—to liberate them from slavery so they could own their own property and could have the personal freedom to worship Him. Thus, God forever connects economics and liberty to worship. *"And God spake all these words, saying, 'I am the LORD thy God, which have brought thee out of the land of Egypt, out of the house of bondage'"* (Exod. 20:1-2 KJV). If God was just a moralist concerned only with inward piety, then He would have left them in slavery and merely told them to walk in the joy of the Lord in their bondage and brokenness.

Regarding the right of an individual to buy, sell, and own property, we need to look at the Seventh and Tenth Commandments, which warn us not to steal or covet property belonging to another. This clearly shows that the Marxist egalitarian philosophy is unbiblical because it opposes the free market and the rights of individuals to own property. Marxism also caters to those who want equality, thus giving in to those who covet the wealth of others who prosper and own property.

This is elaborated on in Exodus 22:1-15, which are referred to as the Laws of Restitution. They are much more humane than the American penal system, which requires a thief to spend a long period of time incarcerated with hardened criminals. The biblical law regarding theft required them to provide ample restitution to the family from which they stole. In cases where the thief couldn't afford restitution, they would be forced to work for the victim as a slave until the debt was paid off. Having a thief work for his or her victim until the repayment of debt is more humane than putting a person in jail wherein they might become a victim of sodomy and be a slave of the state. In Exodus 22:4-15, with regard to their neighbor's loss of property, the guilty party had to restore at least double what they were responsible for.

Please take a moment to read through Appendices C and D to review my thoughts on the Ten Commandments and their application to *Kingdom Awakening*.

The Relevancy of the Law of Moses to the Cultural Commission

Many biblical scholars believe that the ceremonial portion of the law has been done away with, especially with regard to circumcision and Levitical sacrifice. Hebrews 10:1 states:

> *The law is only a shadow of the good things that are coming—not the realities themselves. For this reason it can never, by the same sacrifices repeated endlessly year after year, make perfect those who draw near to worship* (Hebrews 10:1 NIV).

Thus, the grace that came through Jesus' death oversteps the system of Old Testament ceremonial law. Most biblical scholars also agree that the moral law, namely the Ten Commandments found in Exodus 20, is still in effect in the New Covenant.

However, with civic law there are several different perspectives:

1. Dispensational: Their position is essentially one of "antinomianism" or no law, stating that the Old Testament law has been done away with in Christ. All believers have to do is walk in the Spirit because the law of God is automatically written in their hearts.

2. Classical Reformed: They believe that the Old Testament civic law is still applicable in the New Covenant, but that it is modified according to the New Covenant standard of grace. John 1:17 says, *"For the law was given through Moses; grace and truth came through Jesus Christ"* (NIV). The various punishments of Old Testament civil law are no longer in effect legalistically. For example, sexual sins and sins of disobedience to parents are no longer a capital crime, with the exception of the basic form of capital

punishment found in Genesis 9:6 for the shedding of innocent human blood.

3. Theonomy: Those within this position believe that while ceremonial law has been done away completely, the civic law is still in effect except in instances dealing with a particular cultural nuance like in Deuteronomy 22:8. *"When you build a new house, make a parapet around your roof so that you may not bring the guilt of bloodshed on your house if someone falls from the roof"* (NIV). In their opinion, if we don't take this stance, we are left with too much room for human logic and autonomy, and it violates what Jesus said in Matthew 5:17-19.

Do not think that I have come to abolish the Law or the Prophets; I have not come to abolish them but to fulfill them. I tell you the truth, until Heaven and earth disappear, not the smallest letter, not the least stroke of a pen, will by any means disappear from the Law until everything is accomplished. Anyone who breaks one of the least of these commandments and teaches others to do the same will be called least in the Kingdom of Heaven, but whoever practices and teaches others to do the same will be called great in the Kingdom of Heaven (Matthew 5:17-19 NIV).

This being said, there are various views concerning the relationship between the Gospels and the Law of Moses and we are left asking if the Gospels are applying the Old Testament laws correctly, reinterpreting them, or doing away with them completely. Are the Gospels better classified under Old Testament law, New Testament law, or a combination of both testaments? Was John the Baptist an Old Testament prophet or a New Testament prophet? Obviously, these are important questions to ponder since how we answer them will affect how much of the Old Testament we attempt to apply in this present age.

Personally, I believe that the primary basis of dispute between Jesus and the teachers of the law had to do with the Pharisees and Scribes teaching rabbinical commentary and tradition rather than holding to the Old Testament Scriptures.

> *Then the Pharisees and scribes asked Him, "Why do Your disciples not walk according to the tradition of the elders, but eat bread with unwashed hands?" He answered and said to them, "Well did Isaiah prophesy of you hypocrites, as it is written: 'This people honors Me with their lips, But their heart is far from Me. And in vain they worship Me, Teaching as doctrines the commandments of men.'* **For laying aside the commandment of God, you hold the tradition of men**—*the washing of pitchers and cups, and many other such things you do...All too well you reject the commandment of God, that you may keep your tradition. For Moses said, 'Honor your father and your mother'; and, 'He who curses father or mother, let him be put to death.' But you say, 'If a man says to his father or mother, "Whatever profit you might have received from me is Corban"—' (that is, a gift to God), then you no longer let him do anything for his father or his mother, making the word of God of no effect through your tradition which you have handed down. And many such things you do"'* (Mark 7:5-13).

When Jesus actually commented on the Law of Moses, He never did away with it but brought out the fuller and richer meaning behind the letter of the law. For example, in Matthew 5:21, Jesus gives His interpretation of breaking the Sixth

Commandment, *"Thou shalt not murder,"* to include the inward condition of the heart and expression of the mouth (see Exod. 20:13).

> *You have heard that it was said to those of old, 'You shall not murder, and whoever murders will be in danger of the judgment.' But I say to you that whoever is angry with his brother without a cause shall be in danger of the judgment. And whoever says to his brother, 'Raca!' shall be in danger of the council. But whoever says, 'You fool!' shall be in danger of hell fire* (Matthew 5:21-23).

Jesus also taught that breaking the Seventh Commandment, *"Thou shalt not commit adultery,"* was not only the physical act of fornication but an inward desire of sexual lust toward another person (see Exod. 20:14).

> *You have heard that it was said to those of old, You shall not commit adultery. But I say to you that whoever looks at a woman to lust for her has already committed adultery with her in his heart* (Matthew 5:27-28).

I believe that the New Testament is a continuation of the Old Testament, with the exception of the ceremonial law modifications made to the Old Testament civil law. Having this understanding gives me the impetus to carefully read the Old Testament so I can apply moral and civil law to public policy. Doing this also enables me to "get in the game" and follow God's cultural mandate of inheriting and subduing the earth as given in Genesis 1:28. If I believed that the Old Testament is only relevant for its stories and is not applicable today, then I would only have the New Testament template, which would exclude the Ten Commandments. The Ten Commandments have value beyond just salvation, and they benefit *every* society.

> **I believe that the New Testament is a continuation of the Old Testament, with the exception of the ceremonial law modifications made to the Old Testament civil law.**

Having a truncated view of the Old Testament greatly limits the scope of Scripture we can use in utilizing Kingdom principles for every realm of world economic, political, and social systems. In order to truly partner together and unify the Body of Christ, we must have a firm foundation with regard to the effect of Kingdom Law on current worldviews.

Examining the Three Positions

Those who believe the law has been done away with in Christ, also known as the hyper-dispensational view, have no answer for the fact that all of the Ten Commandments have been repeated in one fashion or another in the New Testament. The following list shows the Ten Commandments in chronological order and their rendition in the New Testament.

1. *"You shall have no other gods before me"* (Exodus 20:3 NIV).

   And He said to him, "You shall love the Lord your God with all your heart, and with all your soul, and with all your mind." This is the great and foremost commandment. The second is like it, "You shall love your neighbor as yourself." On these two commandments depend the whole Law and the Prophets (Matthew 22:37-40 NASB).

2. *"You shall not make any graven image of anything in heaven or earth"* (Exodus 20:4).

   Little children, keep yourselves from idols (false gods)—[from anything and everything that would occupy the place in your heart due to God, from any sort of substitute for Him that would take first place in your life]. Amen (so let it be) (1 John 5:21 AMP).

3. *"You shall not take the name of the Lord your God in vain"* (Exodus 20:7 NASB).

   Again, you have heard that the ancients were told, "You shall not make false vows, but shall fulfill your vows to the Lord." But I say to you, make no oath at all, either by heaven, for it is the throne of God, or by the earth, for it is the footstool of His feet, or by Jerusalem, for it is the city of the great King (Matthew 5:33-35 NASB).

4. *"Remember the sabbath day to keep it holy"* (Exodus 20:8 KJV).

   So there remains a Sabbath rest for the people of God. For the one who has entered His rest has himself also rested from his works, as God did from His. Therefore let us be diligent to enter that rest, so that no one will fall, through following the same example of disobedience (Hebrews 4:9-11 NASB).

5. *"Honor your father and mother"* (Exodus 20:12 NASB).

   Honor your father and mother (which is the first commandment with a promise), so that it may be well with you, and that you may live long on the earth (Ephesians 6:2-3 NASB).

6. *"You shall not murder"* (Exodus 20:13 NASB).

We know that we have passed out of death into life, because we love the brethren. He who does not love abides in death. Everyone who hates his brother is a murderer; and you know that no murderer has eternal life abiding in him (1 John 3:14-15 NASB).

7. *"You shall not commit adultery"* (Exodus 20:14 NASB).

You have heard that it was said, "You shall not commit adultery"; but I say to you that everyone who looks at a woman with lust for her has already committed adultery with her in his heart (Matthew 5:27-28 NASB).

8. *"You shall not steal"* (Exodus 20:15 NASB).

He who steals must steal no longer; but rather he must labor, performing with his own hands what is good, so that he will have something to share with one who has need (Ephesians 4:28 BNASB).

9 *"You shall not bear false witness against your neighbor"* (Exodus 20:16 BNASB).

Do not lie to one another, since you laid aside the old self with its evil practices (Colossians 3:9 BNASB).

10. *"You shall not covet your neighbor's goods"* (Exodus 20:17).

Let your conversation be without covetousness; and be content with such things as ye have: for he hath said, I will never leave thee, nor forsake thee (Hebrews 13:5 KJV).

To say that the law has been done away with is contradictory if the New Testament is examined carefully. It is clear that the moral component of the law is still in force in the New Testament. When the New Testament speaks of the fact that the law has been done away with, it is referring either to the extra-biblical traditions of the Pharisees[1] or the ceremonial law that Jesus himself fulfilled and was done away (see Heb. 10:1-14; Gal. 5:2-4).

Overall, the hyper-dispensational position sees most of the Old Testament as merely providing illustrations and examples for our homilies, yet the following verses make it clear that the moral Law of Moses is still in effect:

1. Romans 2:13-16 teaches that the Law is seen as the New Testament standard of judgment by the apostle Paul.

2. Romans 2:17-23; 3:20; 7:7, and Galatians 3:24 show why we need the law to restrain sin in society.

3. Romans 3:31, 7:12, 14, 16, 22, 25; First Timothy 1:7-10; and Romans 8:3-4 all show that saints are to walk in and establish the law by faith in this covenant.

The Reformed Position

The classical reformed position, which I agree with, allows for a more balanced view in which the ceremonial law is done away with in Christ, the moral law is still in force, and the civic law is modified in regard to the consequences for sin. This is the more classic theological position and one that properly connects and fulfills the Old and New Testaments covenants.[2] Many in this position believe that the civic law must be modified so the question then becomes, "How can we follow Old Testament civic law in the context of multicultural and polytheistic nations?"

In the New Testament, the Holy Spirit was given to all flesh, and the priority is to see an inward regeneration of sinners by preaching the Word of God rather than executing those who worship other gods and break the commandments. For example, Jesus didn't encourage the stoning of the woman caught in adultery in John 8:1-8. He offered her forgiveness and told her to go and sin no more.

In the New Testament, the Holy Spirit was given to all flesh, and the priority is to see an inward regeneration of sinners by preaching the Word of God rather than executing those who worship other gods and break the commandments.

In First Corinthians 6:1-5, the apostle Paul challenges believers to partner together and handle civil matters using God's Kingdom standards (and by implication the principles found in the moral and civil law), especially in dealing with inner-heart sins and other sins like gossip, slander, pride, and sexual sins that are indeed grievous but not presently classified as capital offenses with regard to the New Testament application of civic law.

If any of you has a dispute with another, dare he take it before the ungodly for judgment instead of before the saints? Do you not know that the saints will judge the world? And if you are to judge the world, are you not competent to judge trivial cases? Do you not know that we will judge angels? How much more the things of this life! Therefore, if you have disputes about such matters, appoint as judges even men of little account in the church! I say this to shame you. Is it possible that there is nobody among you wise enough to judge a dispute between believers? (1 Corinthians 6:1-5 NIV)

The Reconstructionist Movement

The third and final view is that of the theonomist or the re-constructionist. Theonomy is from the Greek words *theos,* which means God, and *nomos,* which means law. This view states that except for the ceremonial law, there is absolute continuity between the covenants. Thus, while the ceremonial law has been abrogated because of its fulfillment in Messiah, both the moral and civic laws are still in effect in their entirety. The goal with this viewpoint is to eventually have a theocracy reminiscent of Israel that includes civic authority meting out capital punishment in the same way described in the Law of Moses.

Prominent teachers in this camp are R.J. Rushdoony, Greg Bahnsen, Kenneth Gentry, and Gary North. Rushdoony does a masterful job explaining this position in his marvelous work, *The Institutes of Biblical Law*. Bahnsen eloquently presents this position in his work *Theonomy in Christian Ethics*. Taking their cue from apologist Cornelius Van Til, they presume that the civic law as shown in the Law of Moses is still applicable to the nations in the New Covenant. They believe that not following the Law opens the door to human autonomy. The problem, though, if we say that this should be applied in principle, is how do we know where to draw the line? By what standard or what person will determine how far we should go in terms of Old Testament adjudication and punishment for breaking the moral law of God?

The theonomist uses Matthew 5:17-19 where Jesus says He didn't come to abolish the law but to fulfill it. *"Not one jot or tittle will pass away until all is fulfilled."* Thus, they believe that all of the civic law is still in effect. Those in the Classical Reformed category would say this doesn't take into account how Jesus fulfilled the law by modifying it with a fullness of grace not seen in the Old Testament (see John 1:18). Theonomists teach Jesus actually affirmed capital punishment in John 8:1-8, since He didn't say the Old Testament punishment for adultery wasn't still in effect. They argue that He merely stated that the witnesses weren't qualified to carry out the punishment, and they assert that Jesus never once refuted any aspect of the Law of Moses in the Gospels; He only refuted the Herodian and Pharisaic traditions. Classical Reformed adherents may counter and say that Jesus could have found a viable witness if He wanted, but because He was transitioning to the New Covenant, He allowed the ministration of grace to cover her sin and give her another chance.

In terms of pure scholarship, those in the theonomist camp are par excellence and are worth studying because they take the Old Covenant seriously. These ten points summarize the position of theonomic ethics:

1. Since the Fall, it has always been unlawful to use the law of God in hopes of establishing one's own personal merit and justification.

2. The Word of the Lord is the sole, supreme, and unchallengeable standard for the actions and attitudes of all men in all areas of life.

3. Our obligation to keep the law of God cannot be judged by any extra-scriptural standard, such as whether its specific requirements are congenial to past traditions or modern feelings and practices.

4. We should presume that Old Testament standing laws continue to be morally binding in the New Testament, unless they are rescinded or modified by further revelation.

5. With regard to the Old Testament law, the New Covenant surpasses the Old Covenant in glory, power, and finality, thus reinforcing former duties. The New Covenant also

supersedes the Old Covenant shadows, thereby changing the application of sacrificial, purity, and separation principles, redefining the people of God and altering the significance of the Promised Land.

6. God's revealed standing laws are a reflection of His immutable moral character and are absolute in the sense of being non-arbitrary, objective, universal, and established in advance of particular circumstances (thus applicable to general types of moral situations).

7. Christian involvement in politics calls for recognition of God's transcendent, absolute, revealed law as a standard by which to judge all social codes.[3]

8. Civil magistrates in all ages and places are obligated to conduct their offices as ministers of God, avenging divine wrath against criminals and giving an account on the final day of their service before the King of kings, their Creator and Judge.

9. The general continuity we presume with respect to the moral standards of the Old Testament applies just as legitimately to matters of socio-political ethics as it does to personal, family, or ecclesiastical ethics.

10. The civil precepts of the Old Testament (standing judicial laws) are a model of perfect social justice for all cultures, even in the punishment of criminals.[4]

The theonomist camp also understands that they are merely laying out general principles and guidelines, but that these principles, "Leave plenty of room for disagreements in biblical exegesis (for prescriptive premises), observation of the world (for factual premises) and reasoning (for logically drawing an application). Thus theonomists will not necessarily agree with each other's every interpretation and ethical conclusion."[5]

Although I appreciate and agree with much of the theonomic premises, I believe the civic law must be modified with regard to capital and other forms of punishment. I do not agree with their attempt to precisely apply Old Testament civic law because of the Old Testament position of conquest and conversion or their method of protecting and maintaining biblical orthodoxy. The following is a summary of my reasons for disagreeing with theonomy:

1. Israel was a theocracy ruled directly from God through the prophets in visions and dreams, and with urim and thummin; thus capital punishment was meted out under the direct leading of the Lord with very little room for human error. Today, false witnesses and accusations abound, although using DNA evidence to match criminals with their crimes has elevated the quality of forensic investigations but still not equal to the accuracy of the urim and thummin.

2. Israel exercised dominion over the nations through the sword—contrary to the New Testament teaching that the faith is spread supernaturally through personal conversions and not by the coercion or the will of man (see John 1:12-13; 3:3-5).

3. Exodus 22:20, Deuteronomy 12:2-3, and 13:1-10 indicate that all violations of the first four Commandments were met with the sword, so in a sense even the religion itself was maintained and protected by the sword. In the New Testament dispensation of grace, Christianity is never spread, maintained, and protected by force (see John 18:36). This must be especially noted in terms of the cultural mandate in Genesis 1:28-29 where believers are called to have dominion in the created order—not over people—and in Matthew 28:19 where the Church is called

to disciple the nations. The question is, how can we legalistically follow Old Testament civic law in the context
of multicultural and polytheistic nations? In Old Testament instances, when the prophets ministered to gentile
nations, they weren't held accountable to the civic law, but
to the moral law.[6]

**The question is, how can we
legalistically follow Old Testament
civic law in the context of multicultural
and polytheistic nations?**

---

4. Because the Holy Spirit was given to all flesh (as opposed
   to just the prophets and a few others in the Old Testament), the priority in the New Covenant is to see an inward regeneration of sinners by preaching the Word of
   God rather than executing those who worship other gods
   and break the commandments.

5. Some of the commandments regarding civic law had to do
   with specific cultural issues like the regulations for building a roof with a ledge and putting fringes on vestments;
   thus we cannot apply the civic law exactly (see Deut.
   22:8,12).

6. It seems the consequences for breaking the moral law
   of God have been modified with regard to breaking the
   Ten Commandments, with the exception of breaking the
   Sixth Commandment ("you shall not kill"). For example,
   in John 8:1-8, Jesus didn't encourage the stoning of the
   woman caught in adultery. Homosexuality was shown to
   be worthy of death in Romans 1:27-32, but Paul laid out

no definitive plan to execute homosexuals or even judge them in a Christian court of law, as he spoke of in First Corinthians 6:1-5.[7]

What we all must understand and agree upon is that in America, this generation and possibly the next will have to concentrate on restoring the Ten Commandments as the foundation of civic law and the judicial system of our land—especially Commandments five through ten. We will have to leave the real work of the application of the first four commandments to civic law to another generation who will receive wisdom from God once our nation is safely in the hands of godly rulers who want to reflect the Scriptures in all aspects of life.

What we all must understand and agree upon is that in America, this generation and possibly the next will have to concentrate on restoring the Ten Commandments as the foundation of civic law and the judicial system of our land—especially Commandments five through ten.

Theocracy, Humanocracy, or Democracy as Our Ultimate End

So what is the biblical position regarding the influence of God's law on the State? Does God want a theocracy where the church establishes a Christian government? Understanding the various views on this is important because they will determine how we approach our political and economic systems. With most of the American Church mistakenly believing that the Constitution teaches the separation of church and state, a large percentage of Christians are intentionally separating their Christianity from the workplace. The following is intended to help believers come to the biblical position regarding the influence of God's law on the state.

One Position

This first position suggests that Christians should endeavor to influence and direct the political system even if every elected official is not a Christian. Freedom of religion would remain, yet Christianity would be favored. This seems to have been the Puritans' position at the founding of our nation when our country was established as a Christian Commonwealth. With few exceptions, the state constitutions favored a particular denomination, and people could not run for public office unless they identified themselves as a Christian. I personally don't think this is something we should legislate today.

The first four commandments, which deal with a person's relationship to Jehovah, would be modified with regard to the consequences for not worshiping the one true God. However, the Christian religion would still be favored, and there would be laws forbidding business on Sunday, blasphemy, etc. Most importantly, however, there would not be forced conversion, or coercion to convert and punish heretics like in the days of the Inquisition or during John Calvin's leadership in Geneva.

Those in this camp believe in the separation of church and state but do not believe in the separation of God and state. A biblically based meritocracy is when there is a system of government under the influence and using the principles of the law of God, but those selected to lead are voted into office because of merit. They deserve the office because they understand the issues and have solutions to public policy challenges, not just because they have correct doctrine.

A Second Position

Another position is for the church to do all it can to pass laws that reflect commandments five through ten that deal with human relationships, but without the Old Testament system of punishment. For example, the propagation of immoral behavior would be outlawed, but violators would not be punished severely, especially with regard to Old Testament capital offenses. Violators would only be those who intentionally market or promulgate their immoral behavior in public. There would not be Gestapo-like tactics of breaking into the privacy of someone's place of residence to see if laws were being violated. I personally believe this is the best position to take given the current cultural wars. I believe we could agree and begin to influence and move our government in this direction. Once this ground is consolidated, the next generation could then discern how and if they can try to pass laws dealing with commandments one through four.

No Middle Ground

In the end, we come down to a choice between a nation structuring society with biblical laws established by merit, service, and influence, or a society based on humanism, which bases law on science, subjective human opinions, and public opinion polls. There is no middle ground, although the process and the conditions that determine how to reach various kinds of governments are always complex and require multifarious strategies.

We must continue to study what the Scriptures teach about civil law, review historical church/state models, become familiar with contemporary political/social thought, and ask God for His wisdom and mercy as we move toward bringing Kingdom principles to the political sphere. Ultimately, we must trust the Lord to orchestrate His agenda in every legislative hall of the world and to show us how we, as His representatives, are to work together to see that His Kingdom law is to be implemented on earth (see Dan. 2:21, 4:25; Prov. 21:1).

Ultimately, we must trust the Lord to orchestrate His agenda in every legislative hall of the world and to show us how we, as His representatives, are to work together to see that His Kingdom law is to be implemented on earth.

Whether one believes the civic Law of Moses should be modified or should be replicated and applied "as is" to our culture, we should all come to the same conclusion: the Old Testament must be taken seriously and studied in its entirety if we are going to have a biblical blueprint to disciple the nations. I've listed examples of how Exodus 21-23 can be applied to present law in Appendix C of this book.

We need far more than knowledge of Proverbs 13:22 with regard to understanding biblical economics and wealth transfer. We need to have a vast knowledge of both the Ten Commandments and their implications in a civil society by studying the civil law found in the Pentateuch. I've provided a more in-depth study on this in Appendix C.

Think on This

1. If you could dream and have a vision of what society would look like from your ideal, describe it. Imagine that you're a grandparent talking to a grandchild, or an immigrant that could only go so far, but whose grandchild would be fully incorporated into society and live a full life.

2. If we do not partner together to begin to influence the world with Kingdom principles and law, what kind of legacy will we be leaving to our next generation?

3. Read Proverbs 13:22. See Appendix D, "The Blueprint for Biblical Economics."

Endnotes

1. The kind Jesus refuted in Mark 7:1-13.

2. See *Kingdom Revolution,* chapter 3 for a more in-depth study of this.

3. See further explanation of this in chapter seven, "Partnering in Kingdom Politics."

4. Greg Bahnsen, *Theonomy in Christian Ethics* (Nacogdoches, Texas: Covenant Media Press, 2002), xxix.

5. Ibid.

6. Obadiah 1:10; Amos 1:1-2:4; Nahum 1:3-4; and in the Book of Jonah, where the nations were summarily judged for breaking the Sixth Commandment. Judah was judged for breaking the whole law of Moses.

7. Plus the fact that it was categorized with inner-heart sins and other sins like gossip, slander, and pride—sins that are indeed grievous but not classified as capital offenses in regard to civic law.

CHAPTER 7

PARTNERING IN
KINGDOM POLITICS

*And on His robe and on His thigh He has a name
written, "KING OF KINGS, AND LORD OF LORDS"*
(Revelation 19:16 NASB).

One of the most important developments in the Body of Christ since 1980 is the reemergence of the Evangelical church in national politics. The Moral Majority, led by Rev. Jerry Falwell, and the Christian Coalition, led by Rev. Pat Robertson, both had a hand in galvanizing Christians to vote and elect Ronald Reagan to the presidency in the early 1980s. Their efforts have left an imprint on American culture ever since.

Like every movement, Evangelical political involvement has evolved and is continuously responding to the national impulse.

Movement leaders are constantly building on the mistakes and successes of the past and are continuing to mature. Unfortunately, there are still a large number of pastors and Christian leaders who think it is unspiritual for believers to become involved in politics. Those on the left think that religion has no place in public discourse or policy.

Church—a Highly Political Term

When a believer asks me if it is acceptable for the church to be involved in politics, I inform them that the word "church" is a highly political term. The Greek word for church, *ekklesia*, was used before the dawn of Christianity to describe Greek citizens who came together to vote, declare war, and to enact public policy for their cities. The fact that Jesus co-opted this term to describe His followers depicts the nature of the Church as those who come together as a "new congress" to rule as representatives of His Kingdom in culture.

The Greek word for church, *ekklesia*, was used before the dawn of Christianity to describe Greek citizens who came together to vote, declare war, and to enact public policy for their cities.

Furthermore, Jesus' title as "King of kings and Lord of lords" is the most politically charged title a person could possibly have. It means He is the political, religious, and civil President of all presidents and Prime Minister of all prime ministers; the greatest political leader of the world. (See

1 Tim. 6:15; Rev. 1:5, 19:16.) According to Scripture, whether someone likes it or not, or whether one is a Christian or not, Jesus is the boss of every president, governor, mayor, senator, and local leader in the United States and the world. Thus, it is no coincidence that Jesus called His followers the same word Greek citizens used to describe those who came together to make policy decisions.

First Timothy 6:15 says that Jesus is the only true sovereign, which means that He alone is the true Caesar; all other rulers are only temporarily in power and are placed and removed as He sees fit (see Dan. 4:32). Proclaiming the lordship of Christ over all other kings was the primary reason believers were persecuted in the early church and the primary reason Jesus was crucified (see Acts 17:7; John 18:37; 19:15-16). Consequently, Christianity is just as much a political movement as it is a spiritual movement. All believers are really Kingdom politicians!

Understanding this concept grants believers permission to become involved in politics and policy as part of our cultural mandate. In Genesis 1:28, God commanded Adam to have dominion in the created order. In Matthew 28:19, Jesus told His followers to disciple the nations by applying the Bible to civil law, politics, and economics. In Matthew 5:13-16, Jesus called His followers *"the salt of the **earth**"* and *"the light of the **world**,"* not just the salt and light of the church.

Kingdom Politics

As a result of the above concepts, it became a matter of stewardship for me to be involved in the formation of policy in my community, city, and nation. This is why I initiated City Action Coalition, a large multi-denominational association of many churches that has led Evangelicals in the fight against same-sex marriage in the New York region since 2004 and is presently involved in educating and inspiring believers to serve their communities as civic leaders.[1]

Our approach has been one of Kingdom politics instead of partisan politics, because God is neither Democrat nor Republican. Believers need to vote for the candidates who best represent the interests of God's Kingdom instead of sticking to the party of their choice. Our goal is to nurture principle-centered servant leaders who will not compromise their faith for the sake of being elected or staying in proximity to power.

Believers need to vote for the candidates who best represent the interests of God's Kingdom instead of sticking to the party of their choice.

Jim Wallis has been one of the most influential Evangelical leaders to arise in national and international politics and policy in the last 30-plus years. He typically represents both the issues of the left and the right, a different approach than used by past Evangelical leaders, such as Jerry Falwell, Pat Robertson, and the Christian Right. He espouses his nonpartisan views in a best-selling book called *God's Politics*. He thinks that Christians who take policy positions only regarding issues related to personal morality, like abortion and same-sex marriage, misrepresent God and the clear teaching of Scripture. This narrow view does not include social justice issues such as reducing global poverty, feeding the hungry, fighting racism, caring for orphans and widows, or eradicating the AIDS pandemic, or issues such as immigration, universal health care, and affordable housing.

Conservative Theology

While I agree with Wallis' basic premise regarding what the Church is called to engage in, I don't always agree with his ideas on how we are to engage. For example, his *Sojourners Magazine* refuses to take a position on same-sex marriage.[2] He makes statements like "one can also argue for church blessings of gay unions" and "conservative Christians should be careful not to draw their primary line in defense of family at the expense of gay couples who want to make a lifelong commitment" instead of standing prophetically against the cultural, moral, and economic forces that are ripping families apart.[3] "Similarly," he continues, "the controversies over gay marriage may not be as important as the deeper ethical issues of war and the emerging theology of war in American politics."[4] Whether he likes it or not, I believe that making statements like this puts him squarely in the camp of the liberal Christian left.

Wallis has also taken the position that church denominations should not split up over issues of gay marriage,[5] which I feel incredulous about because the church ceases being an authentic Church if it legally and intentionally affirms something that Scripture plainly condemns. Leviticus 18:22 and Romans 1:27 show that the Bible forbids homosexual relations. It is my opinion this would be the same as a pastor getting up in the pulpit one Sunday and announcing to the church that he would now bless couples engaged in fornication and adulterous relationships as long as they make a commitment of love to one another.

The church ceases being an authentic church if it legally and intentionally affirms something Scripture plainly condemns.

Hebrews 13:4 and Ephesians 13:4 clearly state that all sexual relations outside of a marriage between one man and one woman are scripturally unlawful. In Revelation 2:21-23, Jesus judges churches who allow and affirm sexual immorality in their midst. Personally, I affirm the right of conservative Episcopal churches in America to break away from their denomination because of the ordination of gay bishops and the acceptance of same-sex marriage.

Wallis claims to be personally against same-sex marriage but for civil unions. At the same time, he thinks that a good middle ground position for the church is to bless gay unions. This is a troubling position for a minister who claims to be an Evangelical with a conservative theological view of Scripture because, in essence, he is advocating that the church bless what God clearly disapproves of.

Being conservative theologically is much more than just believing in the literal bodily resurrection of Christ: it also means respecting Scripture as the authentic word of God without watering it down based on cultural pressure. Whatever the case, he cannot be a serious theologian with a high view of Scripture if he panders to gay theology or advocates that churches bless gay unions.[6]

Other scholars teach that homosexuality is not really a big deal since it is only mentioned a few times in Scripture. They miss the fact that all sexual sin sits under the general category of fornication and adultery, which breaks the Seventh Commandment and is mentioned numerous times in both testaments (see Exod. 20:14). Logic of this kind is faulty since, if we are consistent with this line of reasoning, then bestiality (having sex with animals) is not a big deal either because it is mentioned less than homosexuality. Jesus didn't mention bestiality, pedophilia, or homosexuality directly in the Gospels because He was preaching to a Jewish audience that already knew and obeyed the Law of Moses. He indirectly alluded to homosexuality when He spoke against fornication in Mark 7:21.

Furthermore, many believe Jesus appeared in a theophany[7] as one of the three men in Genesis 18 who were involved in destroying the cities of Sodom and Gomorrah for rampant homosexuality. Those who cite Ezekiel 16:49-50 to say God didn't judge these two cities for homosexuality but for not feeding the poor are distorting the context. Since Genesis 19:4-11 framed the story to connect the sin of unbridled homosexuality with their subsequent judgment, we have to fit the later passage in Ezekiel into that context. Thus, homosexuals in Sodom were also very self-centered (as their attempted abuse and rape of the two angels demonstrates) and neglected the poor. Furthermore, Ezekiel 16:50 says the cities were also judged because they committed abomination, the very word used to describe homosexuality in Leviticus 18:22.

Politics and Social Justice

I couldn't agree more with Mr. Wallis when he writes:

> God is not partisan; God is not a Republican or a Democrat. When either party tries to politicize God or co-opt religious communities for their political agendas they make a terrible mistake....Both parties and the nation must let the prophetic voice of religion be heard. Faith must be free to challenge both right and left from a consistent moral ground.[8]

Just taking a look at our mission and methodology for the civic leadership training at the end of this chapter shows that we are in agreement on this point. There are good people in both parties, and we need to vote based on biblical principles, not party affiliation.

There are good people in both parties, and we need to vote based on biblical principles, not party affiliation.

The Body of Christ has allowed both political parties to divide the church on ethnic lines. Demographically, blacks in the U.S. vote overwhelmingly Democrat and white Evangelical conservatives usually vote Republican. Blacks vote Democrat even though they are just as conservative as white Evangelical voters when it comes to issues of morality such as abortion or same-sex marriage. Hence, whether true or not, blacks believe the Republican party has been racist since the early 1960s, which has separated the church and stopped black and white leaders from working together politically.

Conversely, Kingdom politics philosophically enables blacks, whites, Hispanics, and all ethnic peoples representing the church to work together to elect the best candidates. Kingdom politics depend on Bible affiliation instead of party affiliation, transcending earthly political identities. Kingdom politics compels the church to be consistent pro-lifers who not only stand against pre-birth abortion but also the post-birth abortion of destiny in areas such as racism, oppression, and poverty. Like Wallis, I think we need to adopt a consistent ethic of life related to all threats to human life and dignity, which makes it possible to have a political platform in either party without a consistent pro-life message or candidate.[9]

I also agree with Mr. Wallis when he says that we can bridge the right and the left together if we would start producing candidates with religious values that don't fall neatly into left and right categories. He sounds like a prophetic sage when he states:

> If there were ever candidates running with a strong set of personal moral values and a commitment to social justice and peace, they could build many bridges to the other side. Personal and social responsibility are both at the heart of religion, and the two together could make a very powerful and compelling political vision for the future of our bitterly divided nation.[10]

I also agree with his assessment that the right is too narrow when limiting their agenda to two moral issues (abortion and same-sex marriage) and the left misses it when mostly Democratic leaders want to restrict religion to the private sphere. When conservatives limit public policy to two moral issues, we represent our God as merely a moralist who is unconcerned with economics, education, the environment, or poverty.

When conservatives limit public policy to two moral issues, we represent our God as merely a moralist who is unconcerned with economics, education, the environment, or poverty.

By limiting religion to the private sphere, the left attempts to have a democracy without a strong moral center that alone can protect our nation's goals of life, liberty, and the pursuit of happiness as found in the Declaration of Independence. On this topic, Wallis correctly states:

> We have been buffeted by private spiritualities that have no connection to public life and a secular politics showing disdain for religion or even spiritual concerns. That leaves spirituality without social consequences and a politics with no soul.[11]

The Poor

In the chapter entitled "The Poor You Will Always Have With You," Wallis' basic exegetical premise is that in Mark 14:3-7 when Jesus made this statement, He meant His disciples would always be in proximity to the poor and outcast. While this may be true in many cases, this interpretation is anchored on the notion that Simon the Leper (the person in whose house Jesus was eating when He made this statement) was both poor and outcast. While the fact that Simon was called a leper might automatically mean he was an outcast because of the way lepers were treated, a case can be made that he must have been very wealthy since he owned his own home. Also, he couldn't have been much of an outcast since his home was in proximity to the city where Jesus and His disciples were going to celebrate the Passover meal.

In addition, people like the woman with the alabaster box of perfume seemed to know who Simon was, as if he had some social standing in the village, and she had no fear of coming inside his home to fellowship with Jesus (see Matt. 26:6-7). Not only that, but there were many others in the house besides Jesus, His disciples, Simon, and the woman, since it says some had indignation, but nowhere does it say that those indignant people were His disciples.

While Mr. Wallis's interpretation of this text may be true, it is conjecture to know for sure whether his interpretation is true enough to support his position regarding biblical discipleship and proximity to the poor. There are many other Scriptures, such as Deuteronomy 15:11, one could cite to show our obligation as believers to the poor. Acts 10:4 shows how important giving to the poor is in God's eyes. There are also many other passages that show how Jesus, Paul, and the apostles targeted the most influential people of society to fulfill their mission—something Mr. Wallis does as well when he tries to influence political and social leaders.

Poverty

I also agree with Mr. Wallis that poverty is related to both individual responsibility and social systems that help trap people in a cycle of poverty. The two greatest indicators of a child's future physical, emotional, and economic success are whether he or she comes from the traditional nuclear family model led by two parents committed to one another in marriage, and whether children have access to a good education. There are numerous sociological statistics that can be cited to prove there is a direct link between stable traditional marriages and healthy children.[12] Society at large acknowledges the need for quality education to break the cycle of poverty.

The two greatest indicators of a child's future physical, emotional, and economic success are whether he or she comes from the traditional nuclear family model led by two parents committed to one another in marriage, and whether children have access to a good education.

I agree with Mr. Wallis when he states:

> Perhaps the greatest scandal of all is the absolutely inferior education that poor children in America are subject to. Because education is so key in changing all the above statistics to rob low income families of the one thing that would most liberate their children is especially cruel and evil. The truth that nobody wants to really say is that affluent American parents would simply never tolerate the disastrous public schools to which so many poor families are forced to send their children. And it is simply not a coincidence that the vast majority of the children in those schools are children of color—mostly black or Hispanic.[13]

Our local church recognizes the twin causes of poverty. In our effort to break the cycle of poverty in our mostly Hispanic community, we focus on marriage and parent-building skills and educating at-risk children through our charity "Children of the City." Our community has a 47 percent high school dropout rate. We know that if we don't aid young children in their academic development, they will have virtually no chance to succeed in life.[14]

So, in essence, Kingdom politics must empower at-risk children and families by teaching them the skills they need to succeed as individuals as well as dealing with systemic injustices such as low-quality public education found mostly in poor ethnic communities. One white leader in our church who serves as a teacher in the New York City Department of Education told me that she once taught grammar school in a poor black community. There were no student computers, classrooms were atrocious, and teacher morale was low. But when she was transferred just a few blocks away to a white neighborhood, this school had first-class computers and beautiful classrooms with high morale among the teachers. This is just one example of systemic injustice that leaders in the Kingdom have to find solutions for if we are going to be the salt and light of the world.

I believe that we live in the greatest country in the world with the greatest opportunities, but there is much more to be done in our urban centers regarding family and education so that the poor have a chance to break out of poverty. Conservatives emphasize individual responsibility and workfare instead of welfare as the key to break poverty. Liberals emphasize public policy and systemic aid. If we are going to make substantial headway in this area, Kingdom politics must include enacting programs using both approaches.

> **I believe that we live in the greatest country in the world with the greatest opportunities, but there is much more to be done in our urban centers regarding family and education so that the poor have a chance to break out of poverty.**

Churches must be willing to step in to aid and connect single parents to the best social services available for childcare, job training, affordable housing, and food. Churches that just offer good preaching and great choirs are not relevant in poor communities that need a holistic Kingdom approach instead of an individualistic, pietistic Gospel.

The International Jubilee 2000 Project

Jim Wallis advocates for the Jubilee 2000 project, which is an international movement to pressure the richest countries in the world (such as the United States, Great Britain, and Japan) to cancel the debt owed them by the poorest developing countries of the world.[15] This is based on Leviticus 25, in which every 50 years the debt of every Jewish person was forgiven and their land returned to them so that every family had a chance to start all over again and not lose their inheritance. While this is indeed a great idea, especially if it frees up monies in developing countries that can be used for health care and education, the biblical idea of Jubilee isn't just some "debt throw away free-for-all" with no ethical stipulations or criteria attached. To be eligible, recipients had to be circumcised, covenant-keeping Jews who believed in and feared Yahweh and who kept the requirements of the Law of Moses.[16] Of course, Leviticus 25 can't be taken out of the context of the whole book of Leviticus or the Pentateuch, which speaks about all the ceremonial, moral, and civil requirements related to participating in Jubilee.

While it may be a good idea to forgive debt, this cannot be done without making certain requirements, especially with regard to dealing with the systemic reasons why these nations are in perpetual debt to begin with. Warring tribal leaders and religious factions between Muslims and Christians actually stop the vast resources of their land from being harvested. Corrupt government officials and civil leaders take the money that was meant to aid the poor and line their own pockets with it!

The early church put forth certain requirements before the poor among them could receive their aid (see 1 Tim. 5:3-16). Those who try to use the Acts 2:44-45 church as a biblical affirmation of the redistribution of wealth miss the fact that those being helped were foreigners from every nation who converted to Christ during the feast of Pentecost. In order to sit under the apostles' doctrine and become disciples, they needed food and shelter (see Acts 2:5-11). Thus, it was the church responding to an extraordinary housing and food shortage caused by the conversion of 3,000 visitors from other lands. This was not the church setting up a normative precedent affirming a socialistic economic theory of redistribution.

Estate or Inheritance Tax

The last concept I want to address is the estate tax. It was originally enacted in 1916 and was meant to affect the wealthiest families to moderate the passing of wealth from one generation to another. The government was attempting to counter the development of wealth aristocracies like those in Europe. The other part of this is the gift tax, which imposes a tax on transfers of property during a person's lifetime. The gift tax prevents avoidance of the estate tax, should a person want to give away his or her estate just before dying.

Besides avoiding the development of wealth aristocracies, the other reason given to justify this tax is that many philanthropic organizations and faith-based groups have supposedly benefited because wealthy people have donated to charities to avoid being heavily taxed. As much as I love charities, I don't think Scripture justifies the legal imposition and coercion of wealthy individuals to support faith-based programs.

Jim Wallis agrees with this taxation and gives Isaiah 5:8 as his reason to justify it. *"Woe to those who add house to house and join field to field, until there is no more room, so that you have to live alone in the midst of the land!"* (Isa. 5:8 NASB) But if we read this in the context of Isaiah 5:7-25, we see that the people being condemned for adding house to house were leaders who wielded their power by shedding innocent blood, and who were drunkards that perverted justice for bribes and rejected the law of the Lord and despised His word. The Amplified translation of this verse adds:

> *Woe to those who join house to house [and by violently expelling the poorer occupants enclose large acreage] and join field to field until there is no place for others and you are made to dwell alone in the midst of the land!* (Isaiah 5:8 AMP)

Using this verse to justify an inheritance tax would be like citing Isaiah 58:6 to teach the church that God doesn't want us to fast from food anymore while we are praying. This is not exegesis but "eisegesis" (i.e., reading into the text)! Thus, this passage does not justify the taxation of wealthy families who are not breaking the law or living like these leaders in Isaiah 5.

Micah 7:3 also suggests that the powerful are not only rich but political leaders. On page 267, Wallis uses a translation that says, "The powerful dictate what they desire thus they pervert justice." I believe this passage actually works against it. Wallis's interpretation in that the inheritance tax still makes the powerful more powerful by putting more money into the hands of the corrupt political system while it disempowers private citizens.

Mr. Wallis not only makes a mistake of biblical interpretation, but he also makes a contextual mistake because he is interpreting this through the eyes of an affluent person in the United States in the 21st century instead of understanding the original biblical context! For example, a person who lived in communist

China or Russia in the 1970s when there were no rich people who could have their estates taxed would have never come to this erroneous interpretation of Micah 7:3!

In my opinion, the estate tax is unethical and unbiblical because the Bible is a multi-generational document in which the godly are called to pass down their inheritance to their children's children so the covenant of God can be confirmed in the earth (see Prov. 22; Deut. 8:18). The Bible teaches believers not to give their inheritance over to ungodly people because they will perpetuate an alien covenant on the earth. This is also the reasoning behind the Jubilee of Leviticus 25. It made it so covenant-keeping people would be able to keep their inheritance and pass it on to their children, not to corrupt politicians and unbelievers who do not keep the biblical covenant.

In my opinion, the estate tax is unethical and unbiblical because the Bible is a multi-generational document in which the godly are called to pass down their inheritance to their children's children so the covenant of God can be confirmed in the earth.

God promises prosperity to those who walk in His covenant. Deuteronomy 28:12-13 shows that God desires His children to be the head and not the tail. The inheritance tax makes the federal and state governments the head and not the tail and financially disempowers families to ensure that the nanny state run by political leaders remains on the top of the food chain!

Finally, the estate tax (before the George W. Bush tax cuts) extracted approximately 50 percent of the wealth of family estates over $600,000. The U.S. national average price of a house today, at approximately $300,000, is basically the same price. Thus, the estate tax robs the middle class of their right to leave their children a home!

Jim Wallis is wrong to support a tax policy that the Word of God condemns in principle and with specific passages. It is a shame that he also tries to justify his position by wresting the Scriptures to make them fit his agenda. First Samuel 8:17 warns of the consequences of any political leader or system that taxes its people equal to the tithe, which should only go to God. How much more will it condemn a political system that taxes and robs His people of their inheritance and is the opposite spirit of the Jubilee of Leviticus 25? In essence, this is double taxation because this money was already "income" taxed prior to the homeowner's death. The state wants to rob the deceased person's family by taxing the dead person's estate again as an inheritance tax!

While Jim Wallis has many good ideas about what needs to be done, I think that many ideas he presents in his book are not God's politics but are the politics of the political left. I only pray that the church will transcend this left-right game and begin to practice Kingdom politics, which is at the heart of the City Action Coalition.

Kingdom Politics in Action

In an attempt to partner together with other Christian leaders, we have put Kingdom Politics in action through the City Action Coalition. Our purpose is to train a new generation of Christian leaders in politics and culture with a biblical worldview for the purpose of promoting a reformation that will encourage societal compassion and transform economics, politics, education, the church, the arts, media, and every realm of society. The glass ceiling has been broken for blacks and women running for president. It is time for the glass ceiling to be broken for Bible-believing Christians in the media and politics as well.

God has given us a vision to launch a nonpartisan, Christ-centered political movement with a ten-year plan to reflect the Judeo-Christian ethos in culture. Our movement centers around five main moral issues: sanctity of life for both the born and unborn; traditional marriage; religious freedom according to the original intent of the First Amendment; opposition to racial discrimination and support for reconciliation between ethnic groups; and support for efforts to practice social compassion through churches and faith-based organizations.

Our goals are to:

- Train 10,000 emerging Christian leaders in the political and cultural landscape.

- Participate in state politics with Christian staff, including interns, political strategists, policy writers, and campaign managers.

- Recruit, encourage, and aid mature Christians to run for local, state, and federal offices and to join local community boards.

- Influence local, state, and federal elections for societal transformation.

- Work for the election of qualified city council members, state assembly members, state senators, federal congressional members, governors, and mayors, especially those who espouse our five main moral values.

- Partner with all people who share our social values irrespective of their religious affinity.

However, a purpose and vision are useless unless we establish a practical and purposeful methodology. God has directed us to train high school and college students from numerous local church bodies. Criteria for trainees includes being members in good standing of a local church with a letter of recommendation from their senior pastor as well as espousing the stated mission, methods, and values of the action coalition. They must also believe that the Bible, in its entirety, is the inspired word of God. They must be humble, teachable, team players, and willing to be coached in the processes as outlined in our training and orientation.

This training will last one year, meeting on a monthly basis. After graduation, certified action coalition representatives will then become part of an action alliance, and will be encouraged to meet several times per year for more training, coaching, and strategizing with key local, state, and national leaders in media and politics. Lifetime coaching arrangements will be facilitated that will match qualified trainees with experts in local, state, or national politics and media.

We invite political, media, and other cultural leaders to invest time into our trainees. We utilize all available resources and partner with other like-minded organizations to accomplish our objectives. We encourage those committed to our process to aid in influencing elections by volunteering their time to campaigns and conducting voter registration drives. We will host candidate forums for those running for office in local, state, and federal elections in a number of local churches or other venues of our choosing. We also train citizens, especially women, traditional minorities, and youth in citizenship, participation, voter registration, and running for election at every level of the political system. Our unique strategy starts as a training center and then expands to being actively involved in political activism, with the goal of dramatically influencing local and state elections.

Our strength is our diversity. Some of our leaders and churches typically vote for Democrats, others for Republicans. Thus, we have not been commandeered by any particular political party and cannot be stigmatized as either belonging to the left or the right. We can aid both Democratic and Republican candidates without compromising our mission. This is because our immediate goal is not to challenge unbiblical public policy but rather, we look toward a long-term plan to infiltrate local, state, and national political systems by placing mature Christians in positions of influence as staff members of elected officials (public policy framers, speech writers, campaign managers, etc.). This will allow pastors to work with local elected officials who may not agree with our coalition on the five key issues mentioned above. We will also set up a coaching system to provide long-term support for those we send out into the marketplace, to ensure they remain faithful to our original mission.

Principle Centered, not Party-Centered

Our mission does not violate the supposed "separation of church and state," because we will endeavor to place individual Christians—not churches or denominations—in government. We believe in the separation of church and state but not in the separation of religious values and/or God and state.

We endeavor to transition the church from being influenced by the Republican or Democratic parties to being the transformer of these parties.

Our coalition will be a principle-centered, not party-centered organization that gathers around the five key issues mentioned above. But we will not seek unanimity on other issues, such as affirmative action, immigration, or even the environment, which could divide us and destroy our mission.

We affirm the ideals and precepts of the Declaration of Independence and the Constitution of the United States of America. As stated in the Declaration, "we hold these truths to be self-evident" that our values, liberties, and blessings come from God and that all men are created equal, with freedom to pursue life, liberty, and happiness. From the preamble to our Constitution, we affirm our right to "establish justice, insure domestic tranquility, provide for the common defense, promote the general welfare and secure the blessings of liberty to ourselves and our posterity."

We stand for the protection of First Amendment rights of religious freedom and the free exercise of our religious liberties for all citizens, churches, faiths, and organizations. We say this in light of recent history to the contrary, as in the enactment of hate speech laws, such as SB 1234 in California, which could today be employed to make it a crime to read certain portions of Holy Scripture, even in our churches.

We value the sanctity of human life from the moment of conception to the moment of natural death. We pledge to cultivate a culture of life and oppose the culture of death all around us. We specifically oppose abortion, partial-birth abortion, stem cell research that involves the destruction of human embryos, assisted suicide and euthanasia in any form, and all other forms of interference with God's created human beings. We affirm that God is the author and giver of all life and that God alone determines the boundaries of the life He has created.

We believe that all human beings, without reference to their ethnic origin, country of birth, race, religion, or sex, deserve respect and dignity as created in the image and likeness of God Almighty.

We aspire to be models of a reconciled community of faith. We therefore oppose all forms of discrimination based on race, ethnic origin, sex, age, or religion. We steadfastly encourage all people to love, not hate, to serve their communities, and to demonstrate their love for their neighbors in tangible ways.

> **We aspire to be models of a reconciled community of faith. We therefore oppose all forms of discrimination based on race, ethnic origin, sex, age, or religion.**

We advocate traditional, biblically defined marriage and oppose the legalization of same-sex marriage in any form or fashion. We believe that God created the institution of marriage as the first societal organ and that the family is His first and primary provision for children, and for the elderly, sick, disabled, and disadvantaged among us.

We believe in the empowerment and encouragement of the family and parents to pursue educational options for children, including partnering with local school districts in the education of children, the formation of charter schools, tuition tax vouchers, homeschool education, and the accommodation and assistance of the same by local school district administrators and staff.

We believe that the greatest benefit for society is free religious institutions—churches, synagogues, and other houses of faith—which promote godly values, peaceful liberty, and freedom from oppression, terror, and violence. We affirm the right of religious institutions with respect to (but not limited to) the "Land Use Act"; the preservation of tax-exempt status under the federal, state, and local government laws, regulations, and cases; and we support the widest possible governmental assistance for faith-based initiatives that add to the common welfare.

Often, success lies in not what you know but whom you know. We endeavor to connect potential high-impact Christian leaders with successful Christians in media, and also with political leaders who can coach them in their journey as world changers. Because of our extensive national contacts, our model serves as a catalyst for other, similar Christian political movements in other parts of the nation and the world.

Think on This

1. Use Genesis 1:28; Matthew 5:13-16, 28:19; and First Timothy 6:15 as resources to answer the question of whether Christians should be involved in politics. _____

_____

_____

_____

_____

_____

2. Define the Greek word for church, *ekklesia*. _____

   To call out _____

   _____

   _____

3. Explain what it means to be conservative theologically.

   _____

   _____

   _____

4. Complete the following statements concerning Kingdom politics:

   Bible

   - Kingdom politics depends on *biblical* affiliation instead of party affiliation.

   - Kingdom politics compels the church to be consistent *pro-lifers* who not only stand against *pre-birth abortion* but also the *post-birth abortion* destiny in areas such as racism, oppression, and poverty.

   - We can bridge the right and the left together if we would start producing candidates with *religious values* that don't fall neatly into left and right categories.

   - "We have been buffeted by private spiritualities that have no connection to public life and a secular politics showing disdain for religion or even spiritual concerns. That leaves spirituality without *social* consequences and a *politics* with no soul."[17]

   - Kingdom politics must empower at-risk children and families by *teaching* them the skills they need to succeed as individuals as well as dealing with *systematic injustice*.

Endnotes

1. See the Web site of City Action Coalition International for more details: www.cityactioncoalitioninternational.org.

2. Jim Wallis, *God's Politics: Why the Right Gets It Wrong and the Left Doesn't Get It* (New York: HarperCollins, 2005), 333-334.

3. Ibid., 334-335.

4. Ibid., 336.

5. Read the dialogue between Richard Mouw and Barbara Wheeler in *God's Politics,* 332-333.

6. Gay theology is a position that attempts to explain away all the passages of homosexuality by distorting Scripture to say these passages are merely condemning practices like male prostitution, gay sex combined with idolatry, a person born a heterosexual going against their natural sexual orientation, or that the Old Testament cultural norms don't apply today. Thus, Romans 1:27 is really speaking against heterosexual men going against their natural genetic orientation by having sex with gay men, etc. For more information on this subject, read Greg Bahnsen's *Homosexuality: A Biblical View.*

7. Theophany—the appearance of God in the form of a human.

8. *God's Politics*, xviii.

9. Ibid., xvii.

10. Ibid., xviii.

11. Ibid., xvi.

12. Read "Do Mothers and Fathers Matter?" at the Institute for Marriage and Public Policy's Web site: http://www.marriagedebate.com/pdf/MothersFathersMatter.pdf.

13. *God's Politics,* 223.

14. View our Web site, www.childrenofthecity.org, for more information on this charity.

15. *God's Politics,* 272-278.

16. Read Leviticus 25:18, which shows there were ethical and religious requirements attached to the Jubilee.

17. *God's Politics,* xxvi.

CONCLUSION

THE POWER OF SYNERGISM

It is my ardent desire that this book has given Christian leaders a greater appreciation and a broader understanding of the Body of Christ from the perspective of the Kingdom of God. Truly there are great riches and great lessons we can learn from each of the models of Christianity we reviewed, irrespective of the differences we may have with them.

Wouldn't it be great if the Body of Christ began a movement that espoused the strengths of all these models and eschewed their weaknesses? By focusing on the strengths, together we could overcome the weaknesses and create a synergistic Kingdom movement of churches in the world as effective ambassadors of Christ but not "of the world," in the sense of participating in what is not acceptable according to Kingdom law. As the unified Body of Christ, we would reflect the incarnation and "humanness" of Christ without compromising His divinity and Word. We would combine efforts to diligently train our youth to serve as Kingdom-minded leaders in society and demonstrate the Lordship of Christ over all creation. As we model the unity and power of the Kingdom of God in the midst of the kingdom of darkness, the world would clearly see the difference and choose the light.

Wouldn't it be great if the Body of Christ began a movement that espoused the strengths of all these models and eschewed their weaknesses?

We all have a responsibility to live out the cultural mandate God has given us. Our faith is not private, but rather it is designed to penetrate every part of this world. The Kingdom of God is vast, and I trust that our study has expanded your understanding of what it's all about.

My prayer for you is that you would have a passion to change the community around you, that you would live your faith out in front of others and see God transform even the most hopeless situations. The Kingdom of God is at hand, and you are called to do great things as a co-laborer of Christ. God bless you as you transform culture with God's truth. It's my hope that this book has challenged you to live your life under the lordship of Jesus Christ.

Appendix A

The Five Models
of the Kingdom

Although the following themes were borrowed from *Christ and Culture* by Richard Niebuhr, the content of this chapter is based on my personal observations, which may or may not be reflected in his book. These observations are not meant to offend any person or group but are generalities rather than stereotypes. My purpose in explaining these five differing models of the Kingdom is to clarify viewpoints so that we can focus on the areas where we can agree, and overlook the areas where our philosophies differ, so we can truly partner together for the advancement of the Kingdom.

A quick summary of the five models is as follows:

1. **Christ Against Culture:** The church is separate from and speaking against secular culture rather than trying to transform it.

2. **Christ of Culture:** The church accommodates Christ and Christianity to culture.

3. **Christ Above Culture:** Christ is Lord above all culture, and the church strives to bring all creation into submission to God.

4. **Christ Transforming Culture:** The church functions as salt and light in every realm of society. Those espousing this view believe that they will never completely change the political and economic systems on this side of Heaven, but that they are called to influence each realm as a witness of Christ's Gospel.

5. **Christ and Culture in Paradox:** There are always two kingdoms existing in the world simultaneously—the Kingdom of God and the kingdoms of this world. The two will never mesh together completely but are to function concurrently until the end of time when Christ comes back to judge the world. Some believe this was the viewpoint of Augustine, Luther, and St. Paul.

We will look at each one in more depth so that we will have a better understanding of the various viewpoints and the Body of Christ's approach to culture based on each of these worldviews. I believe that by understanding both our differences and our common ground, we can more effectively partner to accomplish what God has called us to do in our cities and communities.

> **I believe that by understanding both our differences and our common ground, we can more effectively partner to accomplish what God has called us to do in our cities and communities.**

Christ Against Culture

Although there have been both individual church leaders and Christian movements throughout history that have proposed this position, I want to focus on the more recent fundamentalist movement that began in the Evangelical church in the late 1890s and has continued on to the present day. Typically, these fundamentalists are suspicious of all secular culture and regard it as "worldly." This can lead to legalism in their adherents, with such rules as abiding by a certain dress code, avoiding movies and the theater, or counting the arts as a "waste of time." They don't believe the Bible speaks anything of value to such disciplines, except to condemn them for ungodliness.

As a general rule, this worldview advocates the separation of church and culture. First John 2:15, which says you can't love the world and God at the same time, and Second Corinthians 6:14-17, which warns against being *"yoked"* to unbelievers, are key verses used for substantiating this position. Adherents to this viewpoint also tend to be biblicists, which means that their primary focus is to read the Bible instead of any other books.

Along with this position, they tend to be anti-intellectual. However, this does not mean they are unintelligent. It simply means they usually don't espouse university or seminary education for their children or ministers in training. They tend to be parochial in that many organize their own forms of education, including homeschooling or private Christian schools stemming out of their local church. They usually have numerous Bible institutes, which serve as branch schools for a larger, more credible mother institute. They create institutions because they resent that accreditation is given to schools with curriculum that includes subjects like math, science, and language.

They believe in biblical inerrancy, and many in their ranks believe the King James Version is the only authenticated version of Scripture. Their ethnic demographic is mostly Caucasian, and they are mostly independent and Protestant Evangelicals. They are usually highly sectarian, which means they only fellowship with like-minded believers. They believe Evangelical fundamentalists are the sole arbiters of truth; therefore, they tend to shy away from associating with mainline Christian denominations and groups that are non-fundamental. They are anti-hierarchical in regard to recognizing any titles other than "pastor" in the church. They would not recognize the office of the bishop other than it being another way to describe an elder.

Theologically, they tend to be hyper-dispensational and pre-millennial, with an emphasis on the imminent return of the Lord and the rapture of the church, which is perhaps the main reason for their anti-intellectualism—higher education in liberal arts is a waste of time if the end is near. I have had much contact with this category of Christianity because I attended an independent, ultra-fundamentalist Bible institute. Only the Bible or biblical literature was encouraged to be studied, there was no interaction with culture except to go door to door to "witness," women had no leadership or teaching role unless it was to other women, Pentecostal expressions of the gifts of the Spirit were discouraged, and the second coming of Christ was constantly emphasized. In spite of these shortcomings, they instilled in me a love for studying the Word that I will always cherish.

In terms of morality and culture, they tend to have a very simple approach to public policy. They advocate the need for prayer in public schools and the overturning of Roe vs. Wade. They oppose same-sex marriage, illegal immigration, and globalism associated with the United Nations and the New World Order. Most of their congregants scarcely have anything to say about policy other than the pro-life and anti-gay positions. Some of these descriptions may vary with different churches or movements, but generally they are endemic of the fundamentalist movement and have been for the past 130 years.

Critique of Christ Against Culture

I disagree with the Christ Against Culture position and do not recognize it as being fully biblical. I believe that God created the world, and thus it is not inherently evil. God as Creator cannot be separated from Jesus as redeemer and sanctifier. That is to say, Jesus not only died on the cross as our Redeemer but was also the Creator of the world. Thus, He loves and is concerned about all creation and the created order, not just spiritual things (see John 1:3).

The fundamentalist tendencies of Christ Against Culture are a mild form of Gnosticism, in which the material world is deemed evil and the spiritual world holy. John's Gospel counters this position by beginning that the Word was involved in the creation of the universe, and that *"the Word was made flesh"* (John 1:14). One member of the Godhead not only participated in the creation but also took on flesh Himself. This dispels the notion that God is against the created order! Because culture is part of the created order, we can also conclude that the concept of culture is good.

Satan has perverted that which is corrupt, and it is the job of the church to reclaim culture and to straighten what the devil has made crooked. Instead of shirking the arts, science, education, politics, and economics, I think that the church ought to infiltrate and redeem them for God's glory in accordance with the cultural mandate of Genesis 1:28. The church needs another world-class artist like Michaelangelo, who glorified God through his paintings. We need another Christian to compose a classical piece like Handel's *Messiah* so that the world can enter into worship with the Seraphs and Cherubs. We need another scientist like Isaac Newton who wrote numerous books on theology, and a theologian like Jonathan Edwards, who also wrote a scientific treatise on spiders and nature. The world must see the glory of God depicted in all aspects of the created order—not merely by preaching a truncated view of the Gospel.

> **Instead of shirking the arts, science, education, politics, and economics, the church ought to infiltrate and redeem them for God's glory in accordance with the cultural mandate of Genesis 1:28.**

Christ of Culture

The Christ of Culture view is the opposite of the aforementioned view, in that it attempts to accommodate both the church and Christ to culture. In order to do this, much of Scripture must be compromised or allegorized, with an emphasis on human reason to both interpret Scripture and relate it to society. Those who fall into this camp are generally liberal in their theology and politics.

They tend not to believe in the inerrant, plenary inspiration of Scripture. They believe the Bible contains the words of God but is not the Word of God in its totality, and that much of it is symbolic and not to be taken literally. A large percentage of the laws and beliefs of the patriarchs and apostles are thought to be based on cultural nuance rather than on God's thoughts. Many believe only the actual words of Christ in the Gospels are inspired, and negate much of the writings of Paul. Paul may even be vilified because of his view of male headship and his stance against homosexuality.

Most attend historically denominational churches, including Protestant, Roman Catholic, or Anglican, because they get more out of the symbolism of the Bible than taking Scripture literally. They separate their reason from their faith; thus, many of them may be materialists. They believe in macro evolution and at the same time mystically believe that God had a hand in creating the universe. Their goal is to be a friend of culture the way Jesus was a friend to sinners and the world around Him. Many of their church buildings become the center of the community, hosting concerts and art shows, and are used by community service organizations and support groups like Alcoholics Anonymous.

With the exception of conservative Roman Catholics, they tend to vote democrat and support gay rights, same-sex marriage, abortion, and an economic dialectic between capitalism and socialism. They advocate involvement with many humanitarian ventures, such as fighting against hunger and assisting those affected by the AIDS pandemic in Africa. Recent studies have shown that religious conservatives are the most charitable group in America when it comes to donating to causes that aid the poor and needy.[1] Regarding the Roman Catholic Church, many of its bishops, priests, and congregants disagree with the pope on numerous doctrinal issues.

Church attendance in this category is dwindling because their liberal posture dissipates their Christian distinction, causing prospective attendees to wonder why attending church is meaningful if they look no different than the world at large. Theologically, they tend to be Universalists, meaning that Christ atoned for the sins of the whole world, thus all humankind is automatically saved. I think this is an erroneous view of First John 2:2 and Second Corinthians 5:19.

Although a large percentage don't believe in the deity of Christ, many still hold to a Trinitarian position. Also, some non-Catholic denominations ordain women as priests and ministers, not only because of their liberalism but because they don't have enough men studying for the ministry. Their sermons generally avoid offensive passages and terms like *repent* and *hell,* as well as Scripture dealing with women submitting to their husbands and passages against homosexuality. Many tend to be ecumenical in regard to how they relate to other denominations and religions.

Critiquing Christ of Culture

I believe in the inerrancy of the original autographs of Scripture; therefore, I disagree with many of the points mentioned above. To start with, Jesus was a friend of sinners, but He never compromised the Gospel when interacting with them. He was "friendly" in order to serve His agenda, which was, of course, the salvation of sinners. He didn't fellowship for the sake of fellowship or to meet His social needs, but to transform sinners!

The Christ of Culture position eviscerates or removes much of the Bible because some of its teaching is a reflection of patriarchal bias and cultural nuance. I think Scripture is clear on what the universal principles are and what is cultural nuance. When Second Timothy 2:15 instructs believers to *"handle accurately the word of truth,"* it is speaking about the proper exegesis of Scripture that is needed to differentiate between what should be considered God's universal laws and what are specific instructions for particular cultures.

First Corinthians 11:3-10 is a perfect example of a passage that has both universal principles grounded in creation and cultural nuances applicable only for that particular time and culture. When it speaks of the need for women to cover their heads, it was speaking of the fact that in the culture of Corinth, a woman's covered head was a symbol signifying a subordinate relationship to her husband. This was not a hard and fast rule for all churches in all times, but an example of Paul instructing Christians to honor the symbols of the divinely ordained male and female roles established in every culture.

The idea behind a man not wearing a head covering and a woman wearing a head covering really has to do with Paul protecting the male and female distinctions, so their roles don't get reversed. Men shouldn't dress or act like women and vice versa. For example, if in a certain culture men wore dresses and women wore pants, then a man wearing pants in that context would be a violation of the spirit of these passages and of the Law of Moses, where it says that a woman shouldn't wear men's clothing (see Deut. 22:5).

In regard to male headship in the home, Paul taught this because of the order of creation, not because of culture; thus, it was grounded in creation, not culture (see 1 Cor. 11:7-9). Also, in those days, only female prostitutes had bare heads, thus the need for Paul to teach female Christians to attend church with a head covering.

The Christ of Culture faith-reason dichotomy is a problem, because it implies that Christians need to park their brains at the door before they enter the sanctuary. Faith and reason aren't opposites; rather, faith is the prerequisite to reason, because we presuppose a position before we break it down, interpret it, and apply it with human reason.

> **Faith and reason aren't opposites; rather, faith is the prerequisite to reason, because we presuppose a position before we break it down, interpret it, and apply it with human reason.**

These Christians tend to be ecumenical, which means they usually put unity ahead of biblical principle. Jesus called the church to model unity after the Godhead, which was based on truth, subordination, and purpose (see John 17:21-23). Overall, the general tendency of those who adhere to this mind-set is to water down the Gospel for the sake of cultural accommodation.

This makes no sense because it leaves Christians without Christian distinctiveness and without a Gospel. Why would an unbeliever waste his or her time attending weekly services and paying tithe to a church that preaches that none of those "acts" really matter because all people were saved automatically at the cross? Their philosophy rests on the fact that it doesn't matter if one is a Buddhist, Muslim, or Mormon. Therefore, it doesn't matter if you are a comfortable, lazy, nominally-believing Christian who could care less about practicing a Christian life.

I believe, instead of looking for a minimum commitment to God, we need to look for a *radical minimum* in regard to establishing our faith in the context of church and culture. Erwin Rafael McManus said, "It is not the extraordinary standard but the minimum standard that is the critical boundary in shaping a culture. To unleash an apostolic ethos, it is essential to establish a radical minimum."[2] In other words, instead of trying to figure out what can we get away with and yet still remain within the realm of "Christian," we should be striving to be a true image bearer of our God and Creator.

I received this story from one of my editors, Vanessa Chandler, who said she had witnessed an example of setting and living an extraordinary standard in her own church.

> I go to a church called Expression58, which only began a year ago. It is near Hollywood and is made up of mostly artists and those wanting to change Hollywood for Jesus...One of the pastors preached on purity last night...it was a very strong message for the liberal sexual culture of L.A. His point was that as a single 34-year-old man, he is still a virgin and has never opened up the door to pornography. People often tell him that he must be gay because it's not possible for a man to remain pure like that for so long, but he challenged us that when we get into such a love relationship with Jesus, even though we might be tempted, the "higher" calling keeps us from stumbling because it makes us sick inside to think that we have disappointed Jesus. There is a level we reach with God where the temptations no longer have the same hold over us. God cannot entrust us with leadership if we are not "set apart" from everyone else in purity. Believe it or not, his reputation is gaining so much ground that he was invited to go to the Playboy mansion today to "prophetically evangelize!" Of course, he made sure everyone would be fully clothed first...can you imagine? Because God can trust him with the "higher" standard, He has allowed him this opportunity.

In conclusion, Jude 3 instructs the church to *"contend earnestly for the faith which was once for all delivered to the saints"*

(Jude 1:3 NASB). In their zeal to accommodate culture, churches espousing the Christ of Culture position seem to contend against historic Christianity and even advocate for what I see as anti-Christian behavior.

Christ Above Culture

The Christ Above Culture position squares with historic orthodox Christianity more than the first two positions. The Book of Colossians, which emphasizes the cosmic Christ over all creation, can be seen as the theme of this position. Those in this category emphasize the lordship of Christ over every realm of creation. Their starting point in biblical interpretation is cosmology, which has to do with the fact that the cross of Christ dealt with reconciling the created order back to God and not just individual souls (see Col. 1:20).

They emphasize the sovereignty of God. Therefore, many of them espouse the cultural mandate in Genesis 1:28 and the need for a biblical worldview applicable to every discipline of life. Because they believe Christianity should lead in all of culture, they tend to be highly educated, either formally or informally. Generally, they believe in the inerrant, plenary inspiration of the original autographs of Scripture and in the progressive triumph of the Gospel in their eschatology.

Most of their pastors and teachers have a commitment to apologetics, church history, and the early church creeds. Regarding their larger Christian affiliation, some are denominational, liturgical, or even anti-hierarchical. They preach that the church is to actively engage the culture without being invaded by the values of that culture. The two main methods employed in this are education and politics. They also place a high priority on keeping their children in the faith. Many catechize and confirm their children in the faith and believe in infant baptism for second-generation Christians and forward. Theologically, their essential theme of Scripture is the covenant, which is fleshed out in the context of family, church, and culture.

Critique of Christ Over Culture

This is the position with which I most resonate. I believe the main theme in Scripture is the lordship of Christ over all, which enables me to be culturally aware, relevant, and engaged, without compromising my faith or the Gospel. The very essence of this position is the ascendancy of Christ over all. Thus, cultural accommodation will only take place on issues of minor importance for the express purpose of wisely presenting the Gospel, as Paul taught in First Corinthians 9:19-23.

If there are weaknesses in this position, they have to do with some of the adherents, not with theology. Many in this camp tend to be doctrinally dogmatic, highly intellectual, anti-urban, and critical of those outside their circles. Although I see some hopeful signs, this camp must learn to labor with the universal church and agree to disagree on minor theological issues for the greater good of fulfilling the cultural mandate. Because of their intellectualism, some of this camp have a tendency to read Christian books more often than they act like Christians.

Personally, I would rather be a person whom historians write about than a person who merely reads about history. History chronicles the people of action more than it does the people of letters. The Bible should be read with a missiological lens rather than a theological lens. The history of the early church was called the Book of Acts, not the book of doctrine!

> **Personally, I would rather be a person whom historians write about than a person who merely reads about history.**

Furthermore, many of those in this camp are still Cessationists, meaning they don't believe in speaking in tongues and other gifts of the Spirit as recorded in First Corinthians 12-14. Though I disagree, I sympathize with this position because of some excesses, exaggerated by critics of the Charismatic movement, especially the tendency of a minority of Charismatics to put subjective spiritual experiences above Scripture. Consequently, Christ Over Culture adherents could be left outside of God's plan for world evangelization, because Christians of a Pentecostal or Charismatic persuasion are responsible for most of the present success of global evangelization.

In conclusion, my opinion is that this position is the most accurate theologically and balanced in regard to church and culture. I think that theologians in this camp are among the best in past and present church history.

Christ Transforming Culture

Those with the Christ Transforming Culture position are similar to those taking the position above. Both believe that Christ should influence and transform culture. Both are different from the Christ Against Culture position in that they don't believe all culture is worldly and something from which to separate. The difference between Christ Over Culture and Christ Transforming Culture is that the former emphasizes the covenant theme connecting both Testaments and the law of God as the blueprint to disciple the nations, while the latter only goes as far as influencing culture with revival for the purpose of evangelism. It does not fully endorse the idea that the church should be the primary agent for the Kingdom in exercising leadership on the earth before the Lord returns.

Those in the Christ Transforming Culture category emphasize the church as salt and light. With most, this position has more to do with having influence than with having dominion on the earth. Theologically, they are a mixed group, made up of Calvinists, some fundamentalists, Charismatics, and Evangelicals. Their eschatology is generally classical pre-millennial without the hyper-dispensational approach that emphasizes the last days and the rapture of the church. Those with this position are looking more for a revival and a move of God in this present generation than for a reformation that has a residual institutional effect for generations to come. Some say it's similar to the approach of Edwards, Finney, Wesley, and Whitfield. Many Evangelicals in the United States would fit this position, including Charismatic, non-Charismatic, African American, predominately Caucasian, and Hispanic Evangelical churches.

Those with this general position are numerous, eclectic, and have a lot of zeal. They are involved in the unity movements across America by running pastoral fellowships, concerts of prayer, and leadership summits. Historically, they come out of a classical revivalist Evangelical camp that yearns to see a present move of God and a worldwide spiritual awakening. Some national organizations reflecting this position are Mission America, Wheaton College, and *Christianity Today* magazine.

They typically have some of the largest churches in America, with numerous programs such as community housing development projects, church-owned businesses, credit unions, arts ministries, street ministries, prayer ministries, mission teams, ministry to the poor, and marketplace ministries. They serve their community as a Gospel witness for conversions—not necessarily to reform laws, politics, or economics. They are biblically conservative, believing in the plenary inspiration of the Bible, and have numerous accredited Christian colleges all around the United States.

The Caucasians in this camp vote Republican, and the Hispanics and African Americans are privately conservative but usually vote Democrat because of the negative connotations that the Republican Party carries within their minority communities. They are making significant strides politically in this country but are still lagging behind in influencing the culture via major expressions of media, including contemporary music, film, and art. Many famous Christian para-church organizations espouse the views of this camp.

Critique of Christ Transforming Culture

The strength of those in the Christ Transforming Culture position is that they are open to the purposeful unity Jesus taught in John 17:21-23 and desire to see the reality of God manifest in this present day. They want to be culturally relevant in their churches without biblical compromise. They want to have strong local churches and large congregations that impact whole communities. Their leaders are usually not static, but always learning and implementing new strategies for church growth and renewal. They generally want to combine prayers for revival with an equal desire to transform culture. In their focus and approach, they tend to be action-oriented, pragmatic, and missiological rather than contemplative and theological.

The weakness of this position is that, too often, its proponents don't have a multi-generational plan for cultural dominion the way the proponents of Christ Over Culture do. They don't generally catechize and confirm their children in the faith. Thus, they have limited success with keeping their children in the faith once they get to high school and college. Many independent Evangelical churches have "thrown the baby out with the bath water" in regard to their view of mainline denominations, disregarding many of the good traditions handed down through the centuries, including the practice of catechizing children so they are sound in their faith.

Although many work for unity in the church, these non-denominational, independent churches are generally not connected to the historic church because they emphasize Scripture without the early creeds, councils, and writings of the church fathers. This lack of historical connection has opened the door to the postmodern emerging church movement, which, in its zeal to be culturally relevant, can end up in the Christ of Culture accommodating position.

Often, the prayers and preaching in the Christ Transforming Culture position emphasize experience over doctrine and covenant. Their view of the church functioning as salt and light doesn't go far enough because they don't strive to reorder societal structures for dominion the way those who take the Christ Over Culture position do. Generally, many don't understand how Old Testament civic law is still relevant today, especially regarding tort law, economic principles, and guidelines for civic rulers and governments. Most in this position would not espouse theonomy but would limit the relevancy of the law and the Word of God to its moral laws, like the Ten Commandments. Some of these leaders have an idea about cultural transformation but approach it more from a pragmatic action orientation than from a theological basis. A pragmatic approach gives them quick results without strong theological depth for discipleship and generational continuity.

Christ and Culture in Paradox

The last Kingdom model we will look at is more complicated than the rest because it is gray rather than black and white. This is the model where both the Kingdom of light and the kingdom of darkness are juxtaposed as they are able to co-exist in a dualistic sense, without either of them being radically transformed by the other. I do not agree, but there are those who say that the apostle Paul and Martin Luther fit this model because they never intended to change the overall culture and status quo, but just concentrated on the Church. Paul the apostle dealt with the spirit versus the flesh in his epistles as a primary theme, allowed for the institution of Roman slavery to remain, and advocated submission to secular Roman rulers (see Rom. 13:1). St. Augustine spoke about both the City of God and the City of Man co-existing and functioning together in his classic book, *The City of God*.

Those with this position believe the Kingdom of God is always meant to co-exist with the kingdom of darkness and that complete cultural transformation and the regeneration of the world will take place at the consummation of history at the end of time. Their focus is more on the Church than on changing the world. Theologically, their emphasis is on salvation from the power of the flesh so we can live in the newness of the Spirit. A Platonic divide between the flesh and spirit thus ensues.

They believe that when culture is transformed, it is merely the spill-over effect and not by design, because of the great power of God manifested in and throughout the church. Acts 16 and 19 show that there was a commotion in cities because the Gospel was negatively affecting the living of those soothsaying and idol making. Those with this view always have a paradoxical tension theologically, culturally, and practically between the believer and the world.

Their view on the Kingdom of God is that the Kingdom is not of this world, yet it is ever-present in this world; the Kingdom of God is here now, but not yet fully. Although the Kingdom of God is emphasized and taught in the churches, the cultural mandate to have dominion is not a primary or obtainable goal. Their method of engaging the culture is mostly through evangelization.

The principle of the Kingdom is mostly modeled in the church and individual believers; it is not the goal of believers to intentionally influence public policies to reflect these Kingdom values. In Eastern Orthodox churches, even the altar is imaged to reflect paradise. Although they advocate the separation of church and state, they would not be opposed to civic and community leaders changing the laws to reflect Christianity. Many of these create strong Christian subcultures and communities—a Kingdom within a kingdom.

Among the denominational and liturgical churches, the following is common:

1. Spirituality and allegory are strong in their biblical hermeneutics.

2. Many don't take Genesis 1-3 literally.

3. The sacraments of Communion and baptism are strongly emphasized in their services and among individual believers. Thus, the homily is not the main draw.

4. Many Catholic and Orthodox churches generally function with this model in various nations.

5. They don't "rock the boat" of the laws and culture of a nation. (With the exception of when the Roman Catholic Church functions as a leading proponent of traditional family values and the sanctity of life in modern culture.)

6. They are hierarchical in their churches. As a Christian subculture, they model the Kingdom in their own context. The Roman Catholic Church even has their own state within Rome and a United Nations ambassador representing the Vatican.

Critique of Christ and Culture in Paradox

They are not strong apologetically because they don't intentionally obey the cultural mandate in Genesis 1:28. Thus, they passively maintain the status quo of the culture. Because they live in paradox, they live with seeming contradictions to their faith; thus they don't attempt to rationally defend it as often as those in the third and fourth model.

Evangelicals who generally fit this view emphasize the church and that a believer's main focus should be crucifying the flesh, which can lead to self-centeredness. Theologically, many espouse a cognate of amillennialism, an eschatological position that spiritualizes the thousand-year reign of Christ and many other passages. Because the nature of this hermeneutic is allegorical, it makes it easier for them to live in paradox, tension, and even contradiction in their faith because they separate faith from reason.

Denominational churches in this category gravitate toward a more paradoxical motif because of the symbolism in the sacraments. However, the liturgical emphasis on the sacraments can take away an emphasis on doctrine and preaching. Although they catechize their children, their adherents are trained in doctrine and theology in contexts other than the Sunday church service.

My personal experience in the Roman Catholic Church was that they don't emphasize personal evangelism and outreach.

Their growth usually comes from maintaining a generational loyalty from adherents handing down the faith to their children through catechism training, the sacramental traditions of Communion, baptism, confirmation, and parochial schools. However, one might say keeping your children in the faith is far more important and effective than reaching new people and losing your offspring to a non-Christian belief system. I have no documentation to prove the above; it is just my opinion based on extensive interaction with various expressions of the Body of Christ since 1978. Many individuals, conservative Anglican churches, and some churches in liturgical denominations don't fit this generalization.

Strengths of Christ and Culture in Paradox

Their emphasis on the Church enables them to be focused on creating strong ecclesial institutions. Their liturgical emphasis on the sacraments takes the spotlight away from the Sunday preacher as the primary focus and motivation for people to attend services, keeping it Christ-centered instead of personality driven. Many also have a great model of building strong institutions that keep their young. They serve their Parish communities through charities, legal aid, youth centers, and senior care.

Although Evangelicals emphasize evangelistic outreaches, many prefer this model because it is less intrusive to neighbors, and it obeys the Deuteronomy 6:6-8 mandate to train children and the Matthew 25 model of caring for those in need. Their ability to live in paradoxical tension between faith and reason eschews the Baconian inductive method of ascertaining truth (epistemology) and enables them to hold onto their religion in high school and college when faced with contrary belief systems, although some would criticize this as mysticism or fideism.

In conclusion, my observations are not meant to be dogmatic but merely generalizations that can give the reader a broader understanding of the eclectic motifs of those who claim to be a part of Christendom. I am well aware of the inherent weakness of making such sweeping generalizations, because one can never identify every person, denomination, or movement with pinpoint accuracy.

As an example, the reader may have noticed that I placed denominational churches in two of the five categories, Christ Accommodating Culture as well as Christ and Culture. Although I did this because I see strains of both of these motifs in them, I also realize the apparent contradiction in putting them in both categories. I am aware of the fact that in the macro world of denominations, there are shades of both positions, and even within the same denominations there are differences among bishops and priests who may be liberal, conservative, or paradoxical in their biblical hermeneutic. I can only say that I have done my best to reflect my observations, as feeble and finite as they are.

Think on This

This discussion was designed to give you a better understanding of where your own church body functions and how to partner more effectively with those of differing mind-sets. In light of this information, consider the churches and Christian ministries in your local community.

1. List them and identify their particular "model" of the Kingdom.

2. Reread the descriptions of the five models in this chapter and identify the things you can agree upon with the leaders of each church or ministry.[3]

3. Write a strategy from this that you could use to approach the leaders of each church or ministry and propose a way to effectively partner with them in a community effort to advance the Kingdom of God.

4. Perhaps propose a time line for implementing some of these strategies in the upcoming year. Describe some short-term and some long-term goals.

Endnotes

1. Read *Who Really Cares: The Surprising Truth About Compassionate Conservatism* by Arthur C. Brooks (New York: Basic Books, 2006).

2. Erwin Rafael McManus, *An Unstoppable Force: Daring to Become the Church God Had in Mind* (Loveland, Colorado: Group Publishing, 2001), 203.

3. It would also be helpful to purchase H. Richard Niebuhr's book *Christ and Culture* for his take on these five models (Harper & Row, 1956).

APPENDIX B

EXAMPLES OF MODERN POLLUTANTS—ADDITIONAL INFORMATION FOR CHAPTER 3

Examples of modern pollutants include:

- Industrial smokestacks blow into the air dioxins and PCBs from plastics.

- Plastics we use to wrap edible items leak harmful gases into our food that can cause brain damage, hyperactivity, loss of sex drive, and trigger various cancers.

- Pesticides sprayed on fruit and vegetables are known to cause cancers.

- Metals like aluminum (used to package or line boxes containing food) and mercury can contribute to Alzheimer's disease. Mercury, found in high levels in certain fish and in the silver amalgam fillings dentists use on patients, also causes chronic fatigue, inhibits DNA repair, hinders the function of enzymes, interferes with nerve impulses, can kill or alter digestive bacteria, and can contribute to antibiotic resistance (read *What You Don't Know May Be Killing You* by Don Colbert, page 12).

- Communities using fluoride in their drinking water have higher death rates than communities that use well water (read *Detoxify or Die* by Sherry Rogers, page 20).

Appendix C

Exodus 21-23 and the Law

Disability Laws

In today's American culture, disability laws are attention-drawing since billions of dollars are spent on lawsuits and insurance every year. Extraordinarily, the civil Law of Moses dealt with this issue and furnished us with principles we have extracted for use today. Exodus 21:18-19 teaches that if we physically hurt or disable others, we are responsible for providing care and sustenance until they are capable of providing for themselves and their family.

Law Regarding Abortion or a Forced Miscarriage

Abortion is a hot issue today. Many Christians fail to realize that God treats the unborn child as fully human instead of as a "fetus," the humanistic term. One major proof of this pro-life position from the days of Moses is that the death penalty was allotted to any individual who caused the premature death of the unborn (Exod. 21:22-24).

Law Regarding Slavery

Exodus 21:26-27 teaches that God was against the physical abuse of slaves; chattel slavery as found in the American South was also not biblical. Under such abuse, a slave would automatically be given his or her freedom. God commanded that runaway slaves were not to be returned to their former owners (read Deut. 23:15-16). Thus, God legitimized the principles of the underground railroad in our history with such characters as Harriet Tubman, and extolled the virtues of liberty and freedom as taught by John 8:31 and Galatians 3:28. Jesus came to set people free. He did not distinguish between slave or free in salvation.

Law Regarding Capital Punishment for Negligent Homicide

Capital punishment is still a controversial issue today. It was first set in Genesis 9:5 (prior to the Law of Moses) and ratified again in Exodus 21:29 where the death penalty is given to a person who carelessly allows a violent animal to roam freely and as a consequence has killed someone. (The death penalty is also prescribed for other acts such as adultery, rebellion, apostasy, etc., but was modified in the New Testament, as was spoken of previously in Chapter six.) It carried over into the New Testament when, in Romans 13:3-4, Paul sanctioned the use of the sword (death penalty) to punish evildoers. Thus, contrary to the views of many Christians (including Evangelicals), capital punishment is a biblical position but must be applied in rare cases and by wise people, utilizing all current technological advances to guarantee the guilt of the offender, lest an innocent person be put to death for the crime of another.

Laws Regarding Restitution

The laws of restitution as found in Exodus 22:1 are much more humane than the American penal system, which requires a thief to spend a long period of time incarcerated with hardened criminals. The biblical law regarding theft required them to provide ample restitution to the family from which they stole. In cases where the thief couldn't afford restitution, he or she would be forced to work for the victim as a slave until the debt was paid off. Having a thief work for his or her victim until the repayment of debt is more humane than putting a person in jail where they might become a victim of sodomy and be a slave of the state. In Exodus 22:4-15, in regard to their neighbor's loss of property, the guilty party had to restore at least double what they were responsible for.

Law Regarding Self-Defense

A law forbidding the killing of a thief in the daytime is mentioned in Exodus 22:2-3. The idea here is that since we wouldn't see well enough to defend ourselves and our family with proper skill and aim in the dark, we are not guilty for killing thieves for breaking into our house after sundown.

Laws Regarding the Protection of the Helpless in Society

Laws of compassion toward aliens, widows, and orphans are mentioned in Exodus 22:21-24 and numerous other places in

Scripture. These verses show that the Law of Moses was full of mercy and grace, not just condemnation and judgment. God cares for the poor and needy and expects His people to treat all people the way they themselves want to be treated. A guideline we all know and should live by is to *"Love your neighbor as you love yourself,"* as found in Matthew 22:39, which is also exemplified in the parable of the Good Samaritan in Luke 10.

Laws Regarding Loans to Believers

Laws regarding lending money to a fellow believer are found in Exodus 22:25-26. No interest was allowed to accrue, and their blankets had to be returned to them by nightfall so they wouldn't freeze. These laws show that God's law puts compassion over desire for profit.

Laws Regarding Cohabitation with Those of Different Religious Beliefs

Exodus 22:28 taught that it was against the law to revile other gods. The Founding Fathers of the United States carried this principle over when they guaranteed religious freedom to all. It is because of this that we as believers need to respect other religious beliefs, in spite of our lack of agreement with them or their teachings. Christianity should never be imposed on a culture, but it should always transform a society because of the superiority of its truth and the love of Christ's followers.

Laws Against Perjury

The principle for laws against being a false witness in a court of law is shown in Exodus 23:1. Perjury (lying in court) is a federal offense in the United States. This is an understandable law because when people go against the vows they have made to tell the truth, society breaks down in the sense that justice becomes a hollow term rather than a redemptive action.

Laws Regarding Workfare as Opposed to Welfare

Welfare, as instituted by the ideas of President Lyndon Johnson in the 1960s, set up a socialist structure in which the state government annually paid out billions of dollars to people who said they couldn't find work. This destroyed the self-esteem of many in the minority community and hurt them economically for decades to come!

The biblical principle of caring for the poor always combines compassion with allowing them to work. (The Bible teaches us that if a person doesn't work, neither should he eat! Read Proverbs 6 and the Book of Titus.) The law allowing the poor to work for their food is found in Exodus 23:10-11 and Leviticus 16. This shows that the Bible was way ahead of the welfare reform laws enacted by President Clinton in the 1990s, in which people were required to work before they were allowed to receive welfare benefits. Of course, this principle would also include the gleanings laws of Leviticus 19:9-10, in which owners were forbidden to glean their fields wholly so that the poor of the land could glean and have food for their families. The biblical principle is, if you don't work, you shouldn't eat (see 2 Thess. 3:10).

APPENDIX D

THE BLUEPRINT FOR BIBLICAL ECONOMICS AND THE TRANSFER OF WEALTH

Nowadays, there is much talk regarding the transfer of wealth from the sinner to the saint. Proverbs 13:22 is quoted often but without the proper context: *"A good man leaves an inheritance to his children's children, But the wealth of the sinner is stored up for the righteous."* Once we study the Pentateuch and understand general Old Testament teaching on wealth creation and transfer, we can conclude that wealth will not automatically be transferred to believers in Jehovah, and that thinking generationally is only one of the many requirements for wealth transfer.

Through studying the Ten Commandments, we will find that God has given us a blueprint for biblical prosperity. In Exodus 20:1-2, God reminds His people that He has taken them out of slavery and economic bondage so they could worship and honor Him. The Ten Commandments weren't just given as a moral code for individuals but as a corporate blueprint for national *shalom*, prosperity, and for transferring the resources of the earth to those who will biblically manage the planet.

Commandment One: *"You shall have no other gods before me."* This teaches that the nation and its citizens must base their religious, social, and economic systems only on the precepts and worship of the One True God. This also refers to the fact that a nation must always be grounded to the cause, root, and foundation of the universe; focus and loyalty must always be to Him! Matthew 6:33 brings more light to this. We should never put our business or the love of money before our pursuit and loyalty to God. Thus, while we believe in the meritocracy of the free market, believers must see themselves as stewards of the earth under God to spread His covenant (see Deut. 8:18). This is fleshed out in part by loving our neighbor as we love ourselves, which means we are motivated to create wealth to minister to the poor and empower people to replicate our gifts as wealth creators. Putting God first thus means we are not putting money or capitalism first.

The First Commandment also means that the Church must transition from a rights-centered Gospel (e.g., the word of faith movement) to a stewardship-centered understanding of Scripture in which God releases His wealth to those He can trust to fulfill the dominion mandate. Those who believe that being in Christ automatically gives them the right to be financially prosperous so they can have a nice house and live comfortably have put the symptomatic blessing of obeying the One True God above His goal for wealth creation found in Deuteronomy 8:18.

Commandment Two: *"You shall not have a graven image of anything in heaven and on earth."* This not only refers to worshiping man-made idols but is a command to always accurately reflect the nature, holiness, and purpose of God as His image-bearers (see Gen. 1:26-27). It is troubling to me when I see how quickly believers who believe to gain prosperity go to court and sue other believers, not reflecting the clear will of God found in First Corinthians 6:1. While in church on Sunday they tithe and claim a blessing, yet on Monday they are in court suing another believer or operating their business with a worldly, competitive, cutthroat mentality so they can have more money to continue living a self-centered life that doesn't represent God's ways.

Commandment Three: *"You shall not take the name of the Lord in vain."* This means that as believers we are to honor who and what His name represents. We are to use His name in faith to enact His economic values in our wealth creation activities. This commandment teaches that believers should walk in the most legal authority in the universe because we can use the name of Jehovah for profit instead of in vain or for nothing.

Commandment Four: *"Honor the Sabbath day to keep it holy."* Believers who are business owners should not require their workers to work seven days a week. The Sabbath does not just mean one day in seven. It means taking time off with families to worship God during religious feasts (see Deut. 16:1-17), and taking a sabbatical once every seven years (see Lev. 25:20-22; Exod. 23:12). Christian business owners are guilty of breaking the Fourth Commandment if they don't give their employees adequate time off for vacation and worship. The Sabbath is a sign between Him and us that shows we have faith in Him to prosper us.

Commandment Five: *"Honor your father and mother."* This has to do with respecting and building upon the foundation of your forefathers and parents. In regard to economics and wealth, if children obey the Lord and honor their parents, then their parents will trust their wealth to their offspring.[1] Children who didn't honor their parents in biblical times were disinherited, and in cases of severe rebellion, were put to death.[2]

The story of the Prodigal Son in Luke 15 clearly shows that what motivated the backslidden son to repent and come back home to his family was economics. His economic ability was connected to his father's wealth. If this happened today, the prodigal son may have bypassed his family and gone to the local welfare office for state aid.

Commandment Six: *"You shall not kill."* The command not to kill really means not to murder (killing in a "just" war and in capital punishment was sanctioned by both the Old and New Testaments). Romans 13:4 shows that capital punishment was carried over into the New Testament and was entrusted to civil magistrates. Legalized abortion breaks this commandment and is the new genocide of African Americans. In biblical times, wealth was not only in land but in the amount of children you had (see Ps. 127:3-5). In modern times, the sense of wealth being equated with having children has been reversed. People say they can't have children because they can't afford it. Many parents are in conspiracy to kill off their offspring (abortion) for convenience, thus cutting off potential financial supporters in the future. Because of the lack of generational planning and respect for traditional families, many don't care for their parents properly and have delegated the care of the aged to state-funded nursing homes that operate on entitlements. Secular humanists like Margaret Sanger and Thomas Dewey have argued in favor of changing the paradigm to a one-generational, self-centered society.

Commandment Seven: *"You shall not commit adultery."* A husband or wife who commits adultery divides a family, may cause a divorce, and can cause shipwreck with the inheritance and generational wealth potential they could pass down. Adultery is not wrong because God doesn't want us to enjoy pleasure; it is sin because it divides the loyalties between spouses and destroys the spiritual, emotional, and financial well-being of families for generations to come. Much of the cycle of poverty can be traced to adultery, divorce, or cohabitation without marriage. Numerous studies have shown that the children of one man and one woman committed to each other in marriage have the best chance for economic, emotional, and spiritual stability in their lives.[3]

Commandment Eight: *"You shall not steal."* I think that the present progressive tax structure is legalized theft. First Samuel 8:10-18 teaches that any civil government, religious or secular, that extracts 10 percent or more in taxes or tithes is in competition with God as to who will be the provider and king. If those who own private businesses pay people less than what has been agreed upon or less than their skill demands when they have the money to do so, they are also breaking this commandment. When we undervalue people, we are stealing their dignity and diminishing their calling.

Commandment Nine: *"You shall not bear false witness against your neighbor."* Some say this means not to lie, but this really has to do with bringing false accusations against another in a court of law. Obeying this commandment is essential for the prosperity and harmony of a nation or people group. We can see today that many doctors are going out of business because of malpractice lawsuits; also, the cost of car and homeowners' insurance is going through the roof, in part because of false claims.

Commandment Ten: *"You shall not covet your neighbor's goods."* A prosperous nation or people must base their values on justice and equity. I think the present economic system in the United States is based on egalitarianism, not justice. Egalitarianism is a system in which the state attempts to even the playing field by using policies such as affirmative action[4] and progressive taxation.[5] I think the underpinning for these egalitarian policies is covetous people who penalize success and reward failure. Jesus taught in Matthew 25:29 that God gives to those who have and takes away from those who have not. Instead of taking away from the rich, God often gives to those who already are rich because they are usually the only ones who understand how to steward wealth. When covetousness is integrated into a society, it creates class warfare, division, and poverty. The story of the Good Samaritan in Luke 10 shows that it takes a wealthy person to adequately serve the poor. A poor person couldn't have afforded to lend a stranger an extra donkey, pay for a person to stay in an inn for a week, or pay for his medical needs.

Endnotes

1. In biblical times, wealth was based more on family property and job skills than the currency exchange based on money. God always equates dominion with owning land. In Joshua 1:3, the point of the Israelite Exodus out of Egypt was to give Israel their own property and thus freedom to worship the Lord.

2. In biblical times, capital punishment was given for this because a child's rebellion isolates and separates him from the generational blessing preceding him. Thus the child starts with nothing and is on his own; independence is the same as a death sentence in the eyes of a covenantal God. (Read Deut. 21:18-21.)

3. Read "Do Mothers and Fathers Matter?" at the Institute for Marriage and Public Policy's Web site: http://www.marriagedebate.com/pdf/MothersFathersMatter.pdf.

4. Affirmative action is when a person is given entry into school or given a job because of the color of his or her skin, ethnicity, or gender instead of being admitted or hired according to other qualifications. I think affirmative action is

reverse racism because it has the potential to stop another person from being accepted into a university in favor of someone else who is less qualified but with a different skin color.

5. I think the progressive tax structure in the United States forcibly takes from those who make the most money in order to fund entitlement programs for the poor. In essence, a rich person is penalized for making more money than a poor person because he must give more money percentage-wise to the state. I think the biblical model is a flat tax in which rich and poor both pay the same amount (either the 3 percent poll tax in the Old Testament or the 10 percent tithe).

About Joseph Mattera

Joseph Mattera is the overseeing bishop of Resurrection Church in Brooklyn, New York, a multi-ethnic congregation of 40 nationalities. He is also the presiding bishop of Christ Covenant Coalition. He is the author of *Kingdom Revolution* and *Ruling in the Gates,* and has a Web site for Christian leaders at www.josephmattera.org.

www.josephmattera.org

Other Books by Joseph Mattera

Ruling in the Gates (Lake Mary, FL: Creation House, 2003)

Kingdom Revolution (Shippensburg, PA: Destiny Image, 2009)